The Romance of Small-Town
Chautauquas

The Romance of Small-Town
Chautauquas

James R. Schultz

University of Missouri Press
Columbia and London

Library of Congress Cataloging-in-Publication Data

Schultz, James R.
   The romance of small-town chautauquas / James R. Schultz.
     p. cm.
   Includes bibliographical references (p.) and indexes.
   ISBN 0-8262-1440-1 (alk. paper)
    1. Chautauquas—United States—History.   I. Title.
LC6551 .S38 2002
374'.973—dc21   2002027104

Designer: Jennifer Cropp
Typesetter: Bookcomp, Inc.
Printer and binder: Thomson-Shore Inc.
Typefaces: Chochin, Brighton Light, and Bible Script

Publication of this book has been generously assisted
by a gift from Eugene Davidson.

Frontispiece courtesy of Chautauqua Collection, Pelletier Library,
Allegheny College, Meadville, Pennsylvania.

In memory of

Richie and Eben Schultz

Contents

Prologue

Forty miles north of Mark Twain's hometown of Hannibal, Missouri, is the little college town of Canton, birthplace of two remarkable brothers, Richie and Eben Schultz. Richie was born in 1884 and Eben two years later. Growing up on the banks of the Mississippi, the two imaginative boys were influenced by the lore of the mighty river and the legends of Twain. Together, Richie and Eben fished in the Mississippi and its sloughs just as Tom Sawyer and Huckleberry Finn fished in similar waters to the south.

At a local factory, they watched cutters punch out buttons from clamshells gathered from the river. They listened to the stories of black people who had been born as slaves. They talked to Civil War veterans, and because Missouri was a border state, there were some who had fought for the North and some who had fought for the South.

When they heard the sounds of a calliope, they knew that a showboat had arrived at the riverbank and pestered their parents for tickets to attend one of the melodramas staged by the actors on board. They were captured by the romance of the river and the wonders of the world they had yet to know. As they entered their teen years they began to write short stories and poems, some of which were published in the local newspaper. At age sixteen Richie wrote a series of stories that he illustrated with drawings and bound in leather. With such titles as "The Land of Magic," "The Shipwrecked Orphans," and "Fred Farragut: The Hero of Dewey's Squadron," they were part of what he called his Navy series.

As youngsters they had been captivated by the exploits of Frank
Merriwell, a fictional hero whose adventures were chronicled by Burt
L. Standish in a popular series of books for boys. Frank Merriwell had
gone to Yale, so Richie and Eben set their sights on Yale. For economic
reasons they had to settle on a local college for undergraduate work,
but they didn't give up their dreams of Yale. There was always graduate school. To make it possible, their financially strapped father sold
his buggy and wagon business and with the proceeds moved his family
of four to New Haven, Connecticut, where he bought and operated
a rooming house for students. The two sons thrived in the cultural
milieu of the university and graduated with Ph.D.'s in English literature. It was only natural that they should take an interest in the tent
chautauqua movement that originated in their home territory of the
Middle West and focused on education and the arts, their chosen fields
for a professional career.

Richie Schultz was my father. His brother, Eben, was my uncle.
Both became college professors, Richie at Allegheny College in Pennsylvania and Eben at Culver-Stockton College in his hometown of
Canton, Missouri. For many years they spent their summers touring
as superintendents on the tent chautauqua circuits. As a child I was
fascinated by the stories my father told of his chautauqua travels and
the interesting and often famous people with whom he was associated.
The barnstorming aviatrix, Lady Mary Heath, who established many
world records in the early days of flight; young Edgar Bergen with his
puppet, Charlie McCarthy; explorer Carveth Wells; and a magician
who pulled rabbits out of a hat were among those who appealed to my
imagination and sense of wonder.

Both Richie and Eben Schultz collected a wealth of chautauqua
memorabilia, much of which now resides in the archives of the Lawrence Lee Pelletier Library at Allegheny College. Richie's untimely
death prevented him from writing the book he had hoped to write
about this unique cultural movement. Although other books have
since been published on the subject, I decided to undertake what my
father intended to do but with a different spin. My intention has been
to approach the subject from a personal perspective, focusing on the
human-interest side of the tent chautauqua story. Utilizing as a base
the notes and materials that my father and my uncle had collected,
I delved into the archives of university libraries, state and county
historical societies, and the library of the Chautauqua Institution. I

also gathered additional information from personal interviews with people who have memories of attending the chautauquas. The results were rewarding, producing many previously unpublished materials, including many photographs, which help to bring the tent chautauqua era to life.

The Romance of Small-Town

Chautauquas

1

Origin of the Tent Chautauquas

For almost thirty years in the early part of the twentieth century, tent shows known as "chautauquas" brought a mix of popular education and entertainment to small towns of America from coast to coast. It was a cultural phenomenon that filled a void in the lives of rural residents who did not have access to the array of talent available to city dwellers. The appetite of small towns for a menu of lectures, musicals, and theater became evident as the chautauqua movement spread across the country.

Traveling chautauquas grew out of the lyceum movement that was thriving in the latter part of the nineteenth century and into the twentieth. America was striving for culture, and lyceum lectures became a popular medium for informing the public and generating discussion on the issues of the day. Statesmen, theologians, politicians, authors, and poets were among those who appeared on lyceum platforms. It was a way for them to articulate their views on matters of public concern, and they drew large audiences. For those who would rather listen than read, it was a way of keeping up with the times. They may also have been attracted by the star power of the people of prominence booked into the lyceum halls. Carl Sandburg, Ida Tarbell, Booker T. Washington, Edward Everett Hale, Eva Le Gallienne, and others of their stature were sure to guarantee a packed house. It was a new kind of show business, combining education and entertainment.

The lyceum movement had been pioneered by a crusading journalist named James Redpath. An antislavery activist, Redpath traveled

Chautauqua patrons in Racine, Wisconsin. *State Historical Society of Wisconsin WHi (B53) 328.*

Poet and historian Carl Sandburg. *Schultz Family Chautauqua Collection.*

throughout the south, interviewing slaves and reporting their comments in dispatches to Horace Greeley's *New York Tribune*. Capitalizing on his public persona, Redpath launched a lecture bureau in 1868, attracting such luminaries as Mark Twain, Josh Billings, and Henry Ward Beecher as clients.

Other speakers of prominence learned that Redpath could make their lives easier by scheduling and managing engagements for a nominal fee. Soon the Redpath Bureau was booking the biggest names on the lecture circuits. James Redpath continued to dominate the lyceum business until 1875, when, at age forty-two, he was ready for a change. At that point he turned over the company to two of his employees, George H. Hathaway and Major James B. Pond. Redpath continued as an independent booking agent for a short time but soon returned to journalism. Without James Redpath, the bureau lost some of its vitality and one of the two partners, Major Pond. Under the ownership of the other partner, George H. Hathaway, it continued until 1901, when Hathaway sold a third of the business to Keith Vawter, a third to Crawford A. Peffer, and kept a third for himself. The larger cities and towns could support lyceum programs, but it wasn't until the early part of the twentieth century that Keith Vawter, who by then owned and managed the Chicago Branch of the Redpath Lyceum, came up with an idea that brought comparable programs to rural America. Vawter's concept was a circuit of traveling tents that moved from town to town, offering the same quality of lectures and other forms of entertainment available through the lyceum. Vawter named his traveling circuits "chautauquas," modeling them after the Chautauqua Institution in southwestern New York State.

The Chautauqua Institution, established on the shores of Lake Chautauqua in 1874 as a summer school for Methodist Sunday school teachers, evolved over the years into an intellectual community with summerlong programs devoted to lectures, seminars, and workshops on economic and social issues, theology, literature, science, and the arts. Eventually the institution had its own symphony, opera, and summer theater. It is still one of the most active and diverse cultural centers in America.

Chautauqua is a word originated by the Seneca Indians. Various meanings have been ascribed to it. One authority traces its origin to the Seneca word for "child." In this interpretation, according to

James Redpath. *Redpath Chautauqua Collection, Special Collections Department, University of Iowa Libraries, Iowa City, Iowa.*

Keith Vawter. *Redpath Chautauqua Collection, Special Collections Department, University of Iowa Libraries, Iowa City, Iowa.*

Vawter's circuit chautauqua makes its debut. *Chautauqua Collection, Pelletier Library, Allegheny College, Meadville, Pennsylvania.*

Chautauqua Institution campus during the summer season. *Chautauqua Institution Archives, Chautauqua, New York.*

Seneca mythology, a severe storm descended on the lake when the
Senecas first arrived in the area; one of their children was swept into
the lake by the storm and drowned, and the lake was named after the
child. But there are other definitions for what is generally agreed is
a Seneca word: "a bag tied in the middle" or "two moccasins tied together," either of which could describe the shape of the lake. "A place
where fish are taken out" or "foggy place" could also refer to the lake,
and so could "the place of easy death" or "the place where one was
lost." "Flying fish" is another translation. No one seems to know for
sure, but it is generally accepted that Lake Chautauqua was named
by the Senecas and presents a choice of imaginative definitions.

   Keith Vawter introduced his new concept in Marshalltown, Iowa,
where the first traveling chautauqua program was presented in the
summer of 1904 (see Appendix A). Vawter was assisted in the venture by J. Roy Ellison, a member of his staff in the Redpath Lyceum

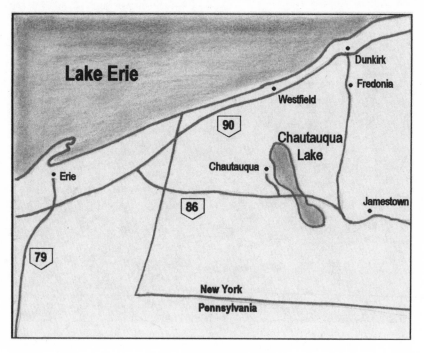

Lake Chautauqua in New York. *Linda and Emily Robinson.*

Bureau. Marshalltown was a wise choice because it had been the site of a small, permanently based, independent chautauqua. It had been a modest success but suffered, as other independents did, from an inability to attract the quality of talent that would guarantee large audiences. With high expectations the movers and shakers of Marshalltown gave a guarantee of two thousand dollars in return for Vawter's services of recruiting and managing the talent.

Vawter and Ellison signed up seven other Iowa towns (McGregor Heights, Iowa Falls, Sioux City, Waterloo, Chariton, Bedford, and Glenwood) for their first circuit venture. Operating as the Standard Redpath Chautauqua, the circuit was soon extended to include four additional towns—Fremont, Fullerton, and Auburn, Nebraska, and Albert Lea, Minnesota. It was not a financial success, but it got the ball rolling for what became a nationwide movement. Learning from his 1904 experience, Vawter restructured the circuit format and, benefiting from an improved economy, launched a more ambitious circuit in 1907. The revitalized circuit, with headquarters in Cedar Rapids, Iowa, covered thirty-three towns in Iowa, Nebraska, and Wisconsin. Although the 1907 season failed again to make a profit, the new formula was a financial success by the following year.

Chautauqua audience in Racine, Wisconsin. *State Historical Society of Wisconsin WHi (X3) 40151.*

Poster advertising the 1925 Redpath Chautauqua. *Chautauqua Collection, Pelletier Library, Allegheny College, Meadville, Pennsylvania.*

A tent chautauqua stayed in a community from five to seven days, offering a variety of cultural events, morning, afternoon, and evening. On a seven-day circuit, chautauqua tents were raised simultaneously in seven nearby towns. The talent that performed in one town on Monday would move to the next town for Tuesday's performance. When the rotation was completed by the end of the week, the seven tents, each with its own crew, were moved to seven more towns in another geographical area. An eighth tent was required to facilitate the move from one area to another. A superintendent was in charge of each of the tents. It was his or her job to work with local officials to assure the sale of tickets, supervise and introduce the talent, serve as a goodwill ambassador to the community, and if possible negotiate a contract for the return of chautauqua the following year. Overseeing the operation of the entire circuit was a general superintendent, representing Redpath's corporate management.

Three weeks before the scheduled opening in each town, the "twenty-one-day advance man" arrived to work with the local chautauqua committee. Over a period of three days, it was his job to generate interest in the chautauqua program and plan the advertising campaign. His visit was followed by the arrival of the "eight-" or

Associated Chautauqua "big top" in Lincoln, Missouri, 1926. *Pat and Bill Kessler Chautauqua Collection.*

"nine-day advance man," who looked over the grounds selected by the local committee and secured permission for the placement of streamers, pennants, and posters. He checked on arrangements for lighting, baggage handling, pianos, and a myriad of other details. When the superintendent arrived two days before the opening, the advance man moved on to the next town.

Vawter's Marshalltown debut presented a five-day program in five nearby towns. After revamping the circuit structure in 1907, he launched a seven-day rotating circuit that became a model for other chautauqua circuits as they were established in other parts of the country. From his headquarters in Cedar Rapids, Vawter eventually operated three circuits under the Redpath-Vawter banner, covering communities in Montana, North and South Dakota, Minnesota, Iowa, and Missouri.

Having multiple performances in tent "auditoriums" provided the economies of scale necessary to attract high-paid talent and put chautauquas on a competitive level with the lyceums. Small towns had neither the financial resources nor the facilities to compete for such talent on their own. Working through the Redpath Lyceum Bureau, in which he held a one-third interest, Vawter was able to recruit big-name talent. He was also able to reduce the costs of advertising and

Commemorative stamp issued in 1974 by the United States Postal Service.

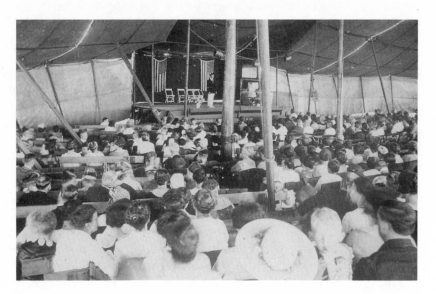

A chautauqua audience. *Chautauqua Collection, Pelletier Library, Allegheny College, Meadville, Pennsylvania.*

promotional materials, much of which could be standardized and shared with multiple communities on the chautauqua circuits. Faced with competition from the circuit chautauquas, locally owned and managed independent chautauquas struggled to survive. Many, such as the one in Marshalltown, were merged into the circuits. A very few—with permanent facilities, sound financial resources, and an established tradition—carried on and are still functioning today. In most small towns, local auditoriums could not handle the crowds that Vawter expected and needed to make chautauqua a financial success. After experimenting with various styles of tents, he resolved the problem by designing a sturdy oval tent, 90 feet wide and 130 feet long, with excellent acoustics, which could accommodate a thousand people.

Using twelve-ounce double-ply canvas, his design provided more durability than circus tents, which at that time were constructed of eight-ounce canvas. In the fiercest storms of summer, the tents might blow down, but by and large they held together. During hot summer nights the canvas sides of the tent were often rolled up to provide fresh air and to take advantage of any breeze. Brown was deliberately chosen as the color for chautauqua tents to distinguish them from the white tents of fly-by-night road shows that didn't measure up to the moral standards of small communities. The town fathers (and mothers) wanted to promote cultural enlightenment and steer people away from the white tents associated with the "evils of show business."

The first tents were lighted with naphtha lamps hung from the center poles. Helen Sandberg recalls how impressed she was as a small child to discover, when she attended the Ellison-White Chautauqua in Woodland, California, that the tent was lighted with electric lamps. The year was 1921, and her home on a ranch three miles from town was not yet wired for electricity. Initially, seating was supplied by wooden benches that folded for easy storage. In an effort to provide more comfortable seating, the benches were supplanted by wooden folding chairs. Most people agreed that even the new chairs were not very comfortable.

Chautauqua tent with ticket booth in lower right and dressing room tent at left. *Chautauqua Institution Archives, Chautauqua, New York.*

2

Growth of the Circuit Chautauquas

Circuit chautauqua flourished in those early days. From its beginning in the Midwest in 1904 it had grown rapidly, expanding across the country. New circuits had been formed and were proliferating. All of the prominent lecture bureaus had developed summer circuits, and new organizations had entered the field. Harry P. Harrison, formerly a partner of Vawter's in the Chicago Redpath Bureau, established his own circuit in 1909 when he and Vawter split the Chicago territory, with Harrison covering states east of the Mississippi to Ohio and south to the Gulf of Mexico.

Capitalizing on his experience as an assistant to Keith Vawter on the Redpath-Vawter circuit, Charles F. Horner also decided to strike out on his own and established the Redpath-Horner Chautauquas in 1913. Starting with one circuit, his organization soon grew to three circuits, serving eight states between the Missouri River and the Rockies. With headquarters in Kansas City, its itineraries covered over three hundred towns in Texas, Louisiana, Arkansas, Oklahoma, Colorado, New Mexico, Kansas, and Nebraska.

With an associate, Clarence White, Roy Ellison left the Vawter organization, also in 1913, to form the Ellison-White Lyceum and Chautauqua Association. With headquarters in Portland, Oregon, the Ellison-White system extended from Canada into California and the Southwest. In terms of geography it became the country's largest chautauqua circuit. The first program of the new organization was presented in Lodi, California, in June 1913. The season closed in

Socializing at the Racine, Wisconsin, chautauqua. *State Historical Society of Wisconsin, WHi (X3) 25079.*

Poster publicizing the 1914 Redpath-Horner Chautauqua in Enid, Oklahoma. *Chautauqua Collection, Pelletier Library, Allegheny College, Meadville, Pennsylvania.*

August of that year in Lewistown, Montana. In 1924, at the height of tent chautauqua's popularity, Ellison-White Chautauquas played in 110 communities in Louisiana, Texas, Arizona, California, Nevada, Idaho, Utah, Oregon, Washington, and Montana (see Appendix B).

Ellison-White went overseas in 1918 to operate chautauquas in Australia and New Zealand, but after seven disappointing seasons, they withdrew. Meanwhile, a Canadian circuit operating under the Ellison-White banner had been launched by J. M. Erickson, an Ellison-White manager, with the backing of Roy Ellison. As soon as he was able to operate independently, Erickson purchased Ellison's interest and renamed the circuit Canadian Chautauquas. He based the circuit in Calgary.

With few exceptions Ellison was able to attract talent of the same high quality as the talent that appeared on the platforms of the Redpath chautauquas in the East and Midwest. The peripatetic William Jennings Bryan and Reverend Frank W. Gunsaulus were among the inspirational speakers who toured the west on the Ellison-White circuits.

The large concert bands were always a feature of Ellison-White programming, as they were on the midwestern and eastern circuits. Salvatore Ciricillo, one of the world's great bandmasters, directed a twenty-seven-piece band that toured on the Ellison-White circuit in 1914. Ciricillo was a dashing showman whose rousing music was consistently acclaimed by chautauqua audiences. Ciricillo was also a composer and wrote "The Chautauqua Girl March," which became a standard part of his repertoire. Ciricillo won renown as a musician while still a young boy in his hometown of Genoa, Italy. He was a cornet soloist of the Genoa Municipal Band when he was eleven years old. At eighteen he became the assistant director of the Fifty-fifth and Sixty-third Regiment bands of Italy.

Another of the big instrumental groups was Thaviu's Exposition Band. It gained international prominence in 1915 when it was selected to play for the opening and closing ceremonies of the Panama-Pacific Exposition in San Francisco. The exposition celebrated the opening of the Panama Canal and opened with an address by Woodrow Wilson. Alert to the publicity value of the prestigious band, Roy Ellison was quick to sign a contract for Thaviu and his musicians to tour on the Ellison-White circuits. Thaviu, who also directed a grand opera company, continued to be a chautauqua attraction well into the 1920s.

Poster promoting the Ellison-White Chautauqua in Elko, Nevada. *Chautauqua Collection, Pelletier Library, Allegheny College, Meadville, Pennsylvania.*

William Jennings Bryan, fourth from left, and local chautauqua committee members. *Chautauqua Institution Archives, Chautauqua, New York.*

A 1914 chautauqua program from Lebanon, Oregon, included this picture of Signor Salvatore Ciricillo. *Oregon Historical Society (OrHi 101420).*

Older citizens and youngsters were given preferential seating at chautauqua performances. *Redpath Chautauqua Collection, Special Collections Department, University of Iowa Libraries, Iowa City, Iowa.*

To garner support for his system, Ellison devised a process that gave local communities a voice in the management. A board of trustees was established in each town, with candidates nominated and selected by a vote of season ticket holders. At an annual meeting of the board, the trustees discussed issues of policy and organization. When chautauqua came to Woodland, California, as it did each year, a contract was signed by the Yolo (County) Chautauqua Association with Ellison-White. It required local sponsors to guarantee the sale of 250 season tickets. A news item in the local newspaper noted that the required amount of season tickets were sold in a matter of hours from the signing of the contract in 1921.

Kenneth Munford, a retired director of the Oregon State University Press, attended chautauqua when it came to Forest Grove, Oregon, seven miles from Banks, his hometown of five hundred people. "Ellison-White Chautauqua had an early impact on me," he writes. While Munford was still a small child, his parents took him to hear William Jennings Bryan deliver his "Prince of Peace" speech at the Forest Grove Chautauqua. He has only a dim recollection of that event, but his mother, in recalling the oration, told him that she was deeply moved by the power of Bryan's message of religious faith and the vivid way in which he described the miracle of growth of "the lowly beet" from a tiny seed.

After Kenneth's father died in 1918, his mother continued the chautauqua tradition, as Kenneth described much later in a letter to a friend: "In the 1920s my mother, older brother, and I regularly attended the weeklong chautauqua at Forest Grove." They made the seven-mile drive in the family's 1924 Overland touring car. "The big airy tent on the campus of Pacific University was an exciting place to be. We did not participate in the children's theater in the mornings, but attended the afternoon and evening sessions."

A highlight of the program for young Kenneth was Chief Strongheart, in full regalia, who told of Indian problems. "Following the afternoon lecture," Kenneth writes, "the Chief stood talking with people in the campus grove. I sneaked around behind him, stalking the mighty Chief, and found to my disappointment that the glorious headdress was just a bunch of old feathers stuck in a belt."

Reflecting on the tent chautauqua era from his home in Corvalis, Oregon, Mr. Munford comments: "Good old chautauqua had an impact in this part of the [Willamette River] valley. Tents, like the one

Record crowds testify to the success of season ticket sales. *Redpath Chautauqua Collection, Special Collections Department, University of Iowa Libraries, Iowa City, Iowa.*

William Jennings Bryan, speaking before a chautauqua audience in Maysville, Missouri. *State Historical Society of Missouri, Columbia.*

in Forest Grove, were set up on the lower campus of Oregon Agricultural College and in Bryant Park in Albany. This pre-electronic enterprise helped to satisfy the hunger for culture which has always been present among Oregon settlers."

Statistics compiled by Charles Horner in 1920 listed twenty-one companies operating ninety-three chautauqua circuits in 8,591 towns, with over 35 million people in attendance. In September 1921 *Billboard* magazine reported that the number of towns visited had grown to 9,875, with attendance reaching 36,576,650. Gross receipts for that year were $9,540,000.

From coast to coast there were few communities, no matter how small, that could not support a chautauqua program during the summer season. Chautauqua's success in rural cities prompted larger cities to follow suit. All America was served. Cities as large as Louisville, Jacksonville, and Cheyenne were served with the more ambitious seven-day programs, while rural villages on the "twilight circuits" benefited from scaled-down programs performed only in the evenings during a three- to five-day run. Even though a number of large cities, including St. Louis, Kansas City, and even Chicago, embraced chautauquas at the peak of the chautauqua movement, the primary support came from the smaller communities having populations of three thousand to fifteen thousand.

The institution was popular everywhere. Throughout the year people looked forward to Chautauqua Week. When it was over, they discussed, criticized, and debated the issues presented by chautauqua's lecturers. The readings by elocutionists were savored by enthusiastic listeners, many of whom preferred the spoken to the written word. The concerts of the musicians and the stage plays continued to be topics of conversation long after the performers and the tent crews were gone. The crowded events of a few days were relived in the lives of the people for months to come.

Chautauqua's appeal was revealed to Ida Tarbell by a woman who told her "It is a great thing for us younger women with growing children. None of us in this town is very rich. Most of us have to do all our work. We have little amusement and almost never get away from home. The chautauqua brings us an entire change. We plan for weeks before it. There is hardly a woman I know in town who has not her work so arranged, her pantry full of food, that she can get to the meetings at half past two in the afternoon and easily stay until five. She gets her work done up for Chautauqua Week."

Large cities, as well as small, embraced chautauquas at the peak of their popularity. *Redpath Chautauqua Collection, Special Collections Department, University of Iowa Libraries, Iowa City, Iowa.*

Chautauqua draws a crowd in Kearney, Nebraska. *Nebraska State Historical Society, RG 2608, 2924.*

Chautauqua program cover. *Schultz Family Chautauqua Collection.*

Keith Vawter expressed the philosophy of chautauqua in publicity materials that were distributed to patrons and guarantors. In 1921 he was quoted in an Iowa newspaper, responding to a charge that chautauqua was guilty of extreme conservatism and catered to the prejudice and intolerance of small towns:

> Chautauqua will continue just so long as we managers keep the middle of the road as to partisan questions and keep ahead of our clientele in thought and quality of programs offered. One of the most indisputable proofs of the educational value of a chautauqua to a community is the fact that an old town demands and appreciates a higher grade of program than a new town. Until today we are most seriously pressed to get a program sufficiently high-brow, or cultured if you please, to suit our old towns, yet carrying sufficient of the best in popular numbers to attract the ever present and much deserving beginner—the family just beginning to distinguish between noise and music.
>
> One factor in our building programs today is a greater breadth of view and broader tolerance on the part of our local boosters and backers, who now encourage, rather than discourage us to book forward-looking speakers who strike from the shoulder, yet who hold different political or economic views on current questions. A chautauqua program is not an expression of personal views, but rather an aggregation of men and women whom we believe to be capable of making us think more clearly, read more widely, sympathize more broadly, yet ever keeping in mind that our clientele include the educated, those not so favored, young and old, keen and dull.

In the same vein, Crawford Peffer, who headed Redpath's eastern circuits said, in his 1920 program circular, "The constant aim is always to include messages of optimism and good cheer, to inspire higher thinking, and by good entertainment to furnish relaxation. But more than all this, each rightly constructed program includes a discussion of some of the great problems about which the people are thinking. These discussions are by specialists who have given deep thought to the problems to be discussed and are intended to help in their solutions."

For the performers, chautauqua offered a respite from the urban pressures of their respective careers. For actors from the New York stage, it provided a paycheck in the off-season summer months. For politicians it was a chance to reach a broader audience and hopefully catch a larger share of the rural vote. For inspirational speakers it was an opportunity to expound on themes to which they were passionately

A varied program for the Brock, Nebraska, chautauqua. *Chautauqua Collection, Pelletier Library, Allegheny College, Meadville, Pennsylvania.*

committed. For some it was a way to advance their careers. For others it was the lure of travel. But there was a downside to life on the road. Small-town hotels were often spartan, and some towns had no hotels at all. Performers were often billeted in the homes of local chautauqua supporters, who offered an abundance of hospitality but not the rest and privacy they would have preferred. Sharing a bath with a family of five could be exasperating. When performing they had to cope with the stifling heat of the confined space of the canvas tent and battle the insects that were drawn by the bright lights.

3

Chautauqua Comes to Town

Following its tenuous start in 1904, Vawter's innovation met with resounding success. Rural communities hungered for cultural opportunities that were rarely available without arduous travel to distant cities. The tent chautauquas brought nationally known speakers and entertainers to the heartland of America where they received an enthusiastic welcome. When chautauqua came to town, residents flocked to every performance.

Macon, Missouri

In Macon, a town of close to five thousand in north-central Missouri, chautauqua became the social event of the year, as it was in hundreds of other communities across the nation. Chautauqua first came to Macon in 1907 and played there every summer into the 1930s. Colorful banners suspended above the main street proclaimed the arrival of chautauqua. When the chautauqua train rolled into town in the summer of 1921, local dignitaries and a brass band were there to give a rousing welcome. Homes, stores, and offices were emptied as townspeople rushed to the station or watched on street corners as the chautauqua caravan moved to Stephens Park, where the tent was raised.

A holiday spirit was in the air as the crowd gathered. Families from distant farms brought their tents and camped out for the full week to be near the center of excitement. They came prepared to attend

Chautauqua tent, front view. *Schultz Family Chautauqua Collection.*

Chautauqua tent, rear view. *Schultz Family Chautauqua Collection.*

the full schedule of programs and watched as the chautauqua parade came into view. Local townspeople arrived with picnic baskets to enjoy a meal under the spreading shade trees before an evening's performance.

Trucks were on hand to carry the large bundles of canvas, tent poles, lumber, folding chairs, and accessories from the depot to the tent grounds. Young men in shirtsleeves and blue jeans, most of them college students, toiled under the hot August sun, driving stakes, raising the great expanse of brown canvas, setting the poles, erecting the canvas fence, putting chairs in place, and setting up small tents to be used as dressing rooms. These energetic young men, known in chautauqua parlance as "the anvil chorus," had become an attraction in themselves. They not only put up the tents, but also sold tickets, ushered, and operated the lighting system.

Although it was discouraged and sometimes forbidden by chautauqua officials, they often dated the local girls. Robert A. McCown, manuscripts librarian at the University of Iowa, estimates that at its peak chautauqua engaged six thousand college boys as crew members each summer. They were paid between fifteen and twenty dollars a week. As the tent was assembled, curious onlookers gathered to give advice, and eager youngsters watched every operation, following the crew with offers of help. After the evening's performance, the dressing rooms often became bedrooms for the tent crews, typically a team of six college boys.

In Macon, with the big tent in place, all was ready. On opening day, people streamed toward the entrance from every direction. Smiling expectantly, townspeople from all walks of life visited with one another as they strolled along, converging on the tent in Stephens Park. To ward off the insufferable heat, many of the women carried parasols and fans. Elderly citizens hobbled along, many with pillows tucked under their arms and some with canes. Children, caught up in the excitement, chased each other in a race to be among the first into the big tent.

The crowd streamed past the canvas box office, through the gateway in the fence, and gathered in the wide area in front of the tent. Before them, the brown big top, the canvas auditorium of chautauqua, rose like a giant mushroom. Confronted with the imposing tent, an awed reporter called it "a huge convocation hall of the University of the Outdoors."

Chautauqua tent, interior. *Schultz Family Chautauqua Collection.*

Schultz Family Chautauqua Collection.

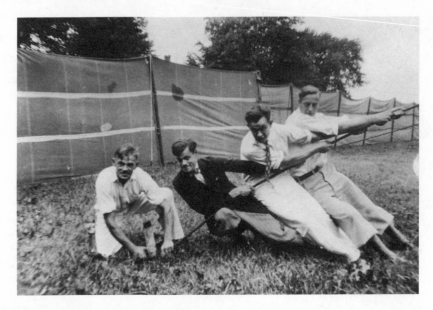

The "anvil chorus." *Schultz Family Chautauqua Collection.*

Near the gate, seated at a table, was the treasurer of the local chautauqua committee, checking individuals against the advance sale of season tickets. Season tickets purchased in advance were $1.50 for the full week of programs. Purchased at the gate they were $2.00. Standing by the treasurer was Eben Schultz, superintendent and platform manager in charge of the week's operation. He served as the official representative of the Redpath-Vawter Chautauqua System in all business transactions, with oversight responsibility for logistics, including talent and work crews. Wearing white trousers, a crisp white shirt, and a straw boater, he smiled a friendly greeting to ticket holders as they passed. Seats in the tent were filling rapidly, fans rustled, and the hum of conversations rose higher.

Eben, noting the arrival of stragglers, looked at his watch and spoke to the committee chairman. Together they hurried to the back of the tent. In a moment they appeared before the curtain to the applause of the audience. The chairman raised his voice in greeting and announced the opening of Chautauqua Week. He then introduced the superintendent. As both men left the stage, there were stirring notes from the piano, the curtains parted, and six girls in colorful costumes swept onto the stage. They were the Redpath-Vawter Sextette, which included two natives of Macon, both of whom later married chautauqua crew members. They began singing the national anthem; the audience rose to join in. Chautauqua was on!

In early summer a newspaper article in the *Macon Chronicle-Herald* publicized the attractions to be featured in the 1921 Chautauqua:

> Quin O'Brien, the eloquent Chicago orator, has announced his subject for this summer's chautauqua, "America's World Leadership." He is considered one of the six greatest orators in America. Farmer Burns, former heavyweight champion wrestler of the world, has been obtained for a talk on good health and its connection to clean living. He is a living example of what clean living can do for a man.
>
> *Broadway Jones*, the well-known New York comedy in which George Cohan starred for two years, will be brought here on chautauqua this season. Carmen Cascova, the brilliant mezzo-soprano who made such a recent hit with the Chicago Grand Opera Company in Chicago and New York has also signed up. Cascova is an Australian and a Pathe artist. As *Musical American* says, "Australia has given to America three great artists: Melba, Percy Grainger, and now Carmen Cascova." Associated with her on chautauqua will be another well-known artist, Florence Hardman, for many years solo violinist with John Philip Sousa, and Stewart Wille, pianist.
>
> Music lovers will rejoice in the announcement of the *Gondoliers*, a musical production featuring eleven artists in elaborate stage settings with lighting effects, costumes, and songs. This company is organized and staged by Arthur Dunham, founder and conductor of the Philharmonic Orchestra of Chicago. A blaze of glory is promised for the final night, which is to be a continuous, rapid-fire affair featuring humorist Jess Pugh, Billy Pryor, the famous black-face comedian, Al Baker, the king of ventriloquists, and Youna, renowned juggler, who will start off the fun.

Planning for Chautauqua Week had been underway for nearly a year. A chautauqua committee of fifty local townspeople had been formed to promote the event and identify sponsors who would guarantee the ticket sales and negotiate a contract with chautauqua officials. The guarantee was fifteen hundred dollars, which required the sale of at least one thousand tickets. Early in the year Superintendent Schultz met with the committee to firm up arrangements and develop the financial support necessary to assure the success of the seven-day

Not far from Macon, St. Charles celebrated chautauqua with its own parade.
John J. Buse Jr. Collection, 1860–1931, Western Historical Manuscript
Collection–Columbia, Missouri.

"Farmer Burns" with Superintendent Richie Schultz. *Schultz Family Chautauqua Collection.*

program. In Macon the enthusiasm for chautauqua was sufficiently high that the full week was sold out by the time chautauqua performers arrived. It was not difficult for Eben to book Macon for a repeat visit the following year. After the final performance, which also closed Redpath-Vawter's 1921 season, the tent was disassembled and taken to the Blees Barn in Macon for storage. It would be shipped to Lake City, Minnesota, the following summer for the start of the 1922 season.

Rachel Miller, a Macon resident, recalled spending the day at chautauqua with perspiration rolling down her face in the oppressive August heat, but "enjoying every minute of the diverse program." Her family always took a picnic lunch so they could stay and enjoy the evening program.

Mrs. John R. Hughes, another Macon devotee, described chautauqua as an opportunity to hear and see national leaders, excellent music, and entertainment. For her the orators were the main attraction. "I gained much from hearing those outstanding speakers of the day," she explained, "because they were able to discuss the important topics in the news. . . . In that time, people could not turn on radio

Jess Pugh was a featured performer on the final night of the Macon chautauqua. *Chautauqua Collection, Pelletier Library, Allegheny College, Meadville, Pennsylvania.*

or television for the latest news." Among her favorites were Senator Robert La Follette and the "silver-tongued" William Jennings Bryan.

Mrs. Hughes's comments reflect the same enthusiasm expressed in her town's 1911 chautauqua program:

> In previous years people of the villages, hamlets, and countryside could only read of great statesmen, orators, and preachers and could only see or hear them by taking long pilgrimages. Now, by means of chautauqua, the best and the greatest talent is brought at insignificant cost to our very doors.
>
> The chautauqua idea is one of the greatest moral and educational forces in the country.
>
> The chautauqua is organized on high grounds and has high aims. It appeals to the thoughtful and cultured and seeks to displace some forms of amusement that are unworthy and fraught with danger.
>
> The chautauqua program will furnish a series of high class entertainments, lectures and musicals which are clean, wholesome, educational and uplifting. You can send your children knowing they will be helped and perhaps receive inspiration that will mold character and channel them into a life of nobility.

Macon's experience with chautauqua in 1921 was not unique. It could have taken place any summer during the first part of the century in any community with a population of fifteen hundred to fifty thousand, in any state, from Maine to California, from Florida to Oregon.

Canton, Missouri

Richie and Eben Schultz were introduced to the tent chautauquas when the Redpath-Vawter circuit came to their hometown of Canton, Missouri, for the first time in 1909. Eben reported the event in an article that was published in the *Quincy (Illinois) Journal.* The Canton chautauqua opened with fanfare on Monday afternoon, August 23. It closed the following Sunday with an evening concert and a presentation appropriate for a Sunday audience, "The Sky Pilot: Missionary of the Great Northwest."

During the week the two brothers and a large percentage of Canton's population heard a stirring lecture by Senator Robert M. La Follette on representative government, and Congressman Charles Landis

Superintendent Eben Schultz (center) enjoys a watermelon break with crew members. *Schultz Family Chautauqua Collection.*

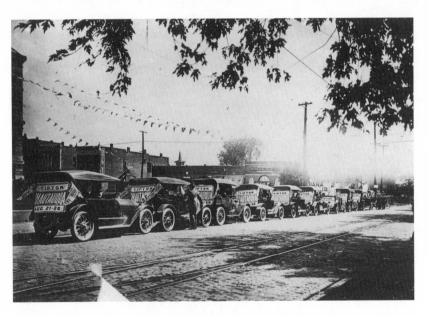

The chautauqua parade was essential for the start of Chautauqua Week. *Redpath Chautauqua Collection, Special Collections Department, University of Iowa Libraries, Iowa City, Iowa.*

delivered a thought-provoking talk on the state of "our merchant marine." Following the lectures were concerts by the Royal English Bell Ringers and the Royal Hungarian Orchestra.

In the mornings chautauqua-goers were given a heavy dose of successive lectures on Christianity: "Christianity as a Moral Force," "Christianity as a Peace Maker," "Christianity as a Reform Force," and "Christianity as a Force for Social Regeneration." Lending additional variety to the week's program was an illustrated lecture on Rome and a concert by the Chicago Boys' Choir. A monologue, "A Message from Mars," and music by a concert trio brought Canton's Chautauqua Week to a close.

Canton became a regular stop on the Vawter circuit and the brothers attended at every opportunity. As a budding musician, Eben was impressed with one of the greatest bands of the day, under the direction of Bohumir Kryl, a world-famous cornetist and former member of John Philip Sousa's band.

Chautauqua made a lasting impression on the Schultz brothers. After completing their education and having taken teaching positions in academia, they were intrigued with the spirit of adventure that chautauqua offered and the opportunity to supplement their professorial salaries. In 1918 both of them signed with the Redpath-Vawter System to spend their summers as chautauqua superintendents. For Eben it was a portentous decision because it was on chautauqua that he met his future bride. As college professors the two brothers found many kindred associates among other chautauqua superintendents who had been recruited from college faculties. When Richie became general superintendent of Redpath Chautauquas of New York and New England, he recruited two additional members of the Allegheny College faculty as superintendents. As a result of the Allegheny connection, a number of Allegheny students spent their summers as chautauqua crew members.

Mt. Pleasant, Iowa

Wesley Coe grew up on a farm near Mt. Pleasant, Iowa, a farming town of thirty-five hundred people. His mother was a schoolteacher and believed in exposing her children to culture. Chautauqua provided that opportunity. When chautauqua came to Mt. Pleasant, as it

Eben Schultz, 1912. *Schultz Family Chautauqua Collection.*

Richie Schultz, 1912. *Schultz Family Chautauqua Collection.*

Chautauqua poster advertising Bohumir Kryl and his band in Albany, Missouri, 1915. *Chautauqua Collection, Pelletier Library, Allegheny College, Meadville, Pennsylvania.*

did in August of every year, Mrs. Coe gathered up her family, packed a picnic lunch, and headed for a park close to the big chautauqua tent. Her interests centered on inspirational talks and travelogues, some of which recounted the adventurous experiences of foreign missionaries. Wesley was impressed by what he heard, but he remembers most clearly the musical events. String quartets were popular in those days, and brass bands were one of his favorites. He was inspired to take clarinet lessons after listening to these ensembles performing in chautauqua, and his love for the clarinet continued through high school and college.

One evening when a violent storm thundered into town, the Coe family was so absorbed by the chautauqua program that they sat firmly in their seats while most of the patrons headed for the exits. The tent remained standing, justifying the Coes' confidence and appreciation for the musicians on the stage.

Portal, North Dakota

In his first assignment with the Redpath-Vawter circuit, Eben Schultz was dispatched to the Canadian border to take charge of Chautauqua Week in Portal, North Dakota. The year was 1918. He arrived in Portal two weeks in advance of the tent crew and performers to check on details of the one-week run.

Shortly after Eben arrived in Portal, he received a letter from his general superintendent, Frank Johnson, on whom he had been counting for advice, saying that he was leaving the circuit to entrain for military camp. World War I was draining off some of chautauqua's most able administrators and some of the performing talent. In his letter, Johnson commented, "When this cruel war is over, our paths may again cross."

Portal attracted a portion of its audience from North Portal, across the border in Saskatchewan, Canada. In keeping with the patriotic tenor of chautauqua, it was customary to open each session with the national anthem. Led by one of the performers, the audience sang loudly and lustily. In the traveling chautauqua era, "America" (also known as "My Country 'Tis of Thee") served as the national anthem. It was not until 1931 that Congress officially established "The Star-Spangled Banner" as the country's anthem. Because of the large Cana-

Die-hard patrons remain seated in a storm-damaged tent. *Schultz Family Chautauqua Collection.*

dian contingent in Portal's chautauqua audience, Eben made sure that "America" was followed with a rendition of "God Save the King."

The war raging in Europe was on everyone's mind, and it was reflected in the programming. Speaking from the chautauqua platform, Dr. E. T. Hagerman lectured on the "trend of the peoples of the world toward democracy." "The terrible conflict on the battlefields of Europe," he said, "is being fought between the forces of autocracy and democracy." "Government should exist for the individual and the individual for the government." An interlude of music by the Chicago Festival Octette followed his presentation. When it concluded, Dr. Hagerman triumphantly announced that he had just received a wire stating that the "Crown Prince and his entire army had just been captured by the Allies." Hearing this bit of what could be termed overblown rhetoric, the audience and the musicians "went wild."

Later in the week, V. E. Shirley delivered a message that told of the achievements of the army and navy and the patriotism through sacrifices by the "folks at home." Reflecting the anti-German sentiment

Chautauqua programs in 1917–1918 reflected a wartime focus. *Chautauqua Collection, Pelletier Library, Allegheny College, Meadville, Pennsylvania.*

that prevailed at the time, he further stated: "The huns and the pro-Germans had better watch out when the boys come home. It may be necessary for them to seek a more congenial climate."

On a more subdued note, "woodsman, poet, and lecturer" Lew R. Sarett described his adventures in the forests of Minnesota and Canada. Reading from his poetry about the wildlife and Indians he encountered, he commanded the attention of an appreciative audience. It was rare for poets to be featured on the chautauqua stage, but Sarett became a star attraction.

Sarett's career was one of variety and color. A professor at Northwestern University, he gained a national reputation, not only as a poet, but also as an entertaining speaker. Occasionally in the summers he worked as a National Park ranger and as a guide in the forests of Minnesota and Canada. It was said that he brought much of the feeling of the outdoors into his poetry. During the week in Portal, he dined with Eben Schultz in a restaurant of the Soo Line Railroad where they ate broiled salmon. At the end of the meal, Sarett read "a little poem about the prairie," which was later published as "Vastness" in one of his books.

It was in Portal that a big storm blew down the tent just prior to a performance of *The Melting Pot,* one of chautauqua's most popular stage plays. In the tradition of "the show must go on," the drama was staged in the open air, a considerable handicap for both the actors and the audience. Subsequent performances were moved to the local high school auditorium.

It was Eben's first experience with storm damage but not the last. The following year his tent blew down in Clermont, Iowa, and the performances were moved to an opera house. Torrential rains sometimes pounded the chautauqua tents to such an extent that excess water collected on the canvas rooftops and had to be drained off so that the tents would not collapse. Fortunately, the storms or the threat of storms did not deter ticket holders from attending the shows and getting their money's worth. To cope with inclement weather, there was usually a "weather committee" in each chautauqua town. A tornado once destroyed a Redpath-Vawter tent in Woodbine, Iowa, but acting on advice from the weather committee, the audience had left the tent before the tornado swept into the town.

F. C. Hoyt, editor of the *International,* Portal's self-described "Home Grown Newspaper," wrote the following in response to a letter he received from Eben in January 1919:

Poet, woodsman, and lecturer Lew Sarett. *Chautauqua
Collection, Pelletier Library, Allegheny College, Meadville,
Pennsylvania.*

Storm-damaged chautauqua tent in Naples, New York. *Chautauqua Collection, Pelletier Library, Allegheny College, Meadville, Pennsylvania.*

You have often been in my thoughts since you were here last summer. I will always connect you with chautauquas and the good work they are doing.

I agree with you, the Portal people are the real sort. The way they have met every war obligation is immense. There are no people this side of heaven that have bigger hearts; giving has become second-nature to them. (I must stop bragging about Portal or I won't have room for other matters.)

So you have been doing your bit in helping to educate the soldier boys. Your work must be very interesting, I am sure. I hope you will be routed up here next summer. You will always find the latch string out at the "famous printing office."

Before he left town Eben was successful in signing twenty-five endorsers for a 1919 contract, assuring the return of chautauqua for another year.

Farmington, Maine

Chautauqua came to Farmington, Maine, for the first time in September 1916. Its debut was accompanied by a flood of publicity in the local newspapers. A press release heralded the arrival of chautauqua

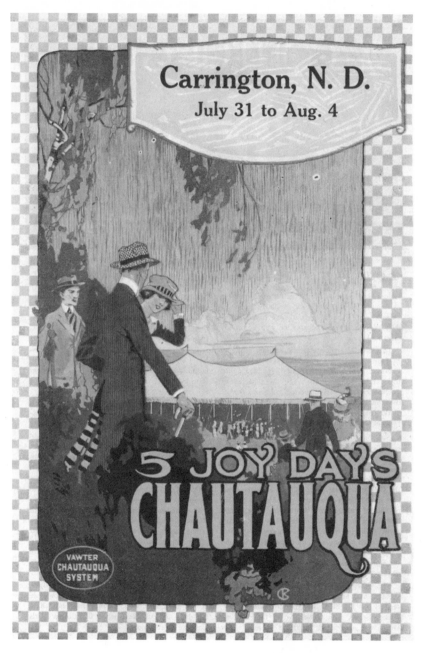

Chautauqua program from the Carrington, North Dakota, chautauqua. *Schultz Family Chautauqua Collection.*

Eben Schultz (right) and chautauqua performers. *Schultz Family Chautauqua Collection.*

with words designed to entice the whole family: "Chautauqua Week is a gala time for everybody from the youngest kiddie to the oldest grownup. Why not make it your homecoming week? Invite your friends and relatives to help you share the six big days of entertainment."

Chautauqua pulled out all the stops to sell tickets for its Farmington debut. As each worker sold a ticket, the good news was telephoned to the county clerk of courts, Byron Small. Small, in turn, saw to it that the courthouse bell was rung to celebrate the transaction. Reporting on this piece of Farmington history, Dick Mallett commented that "the connection between the sale of chautauqua tickets and county affairs was never made clear."

Yet ticket sales were crucial to the financial success of chautauqua programs, and promoters were ingenious in their efforts to assure record attendance. In Perry, New York, a town of forty-five hundred people, the sale of a season ticket was heralded with a single tap of the fire bell in City Hall. And Crawford Peffer, who headed the Redpath

Season tickets for sale. *Chautauqua Collection, Pelletier Library, Allegheny College, Meadville, Pennsylvania.*

chautauquas of New York and New England, at one time enlisted his daughter Nancy to attract season ticket buyers.

Promoting chautauqua in Farmington was the local chautauqua committee of leading citizens. Among them was Dr. W. G. Mallett, president of Farmington State Normal College (now the Farmington campus of the University of Maine). Dr. Mallett's son Dick has a clear recollection of chautauqua. As a seven-year-old, he attended many of the programs of the opening season, and he continued to attend each year until 1932, when chautauqua paid its last visit to Farmington. Dick for the most part eschewed the offerings of Junior Chautauqua for band music and platform lectures. His favorite chautauqua program was the stage band of Jaroslav Cimera, one of the great trombone players, who had formerly played with John Philip Sousa and later formed his own band.

Dick Mallett delights in telling the story of an encounter he had as a nine-year-old while attending chautauqua in 1918. A lecture, judged to be too boring for children, had been scheduled for an afternoon session, so those twelve and under were invited for a swim and corn roast at a nearby swimming hole in the Sandy River. On the way he fell in step with a personable man who engaged him in conversation about his interests and hopes for the future. Dick discovered that, when it came to music, they were on the same wavelength. His new friend played the alto horn and had played in a band. As Dick tells the story, "sometime after we arrived at the swimming hole we were told that the corn roast would be held on the opposite side of the river. This announcement filled me with dismay because I couldn't swim. Hearing of my distress my friend offered to ferry me over the short distance. I was to put my hands on his shoulders, so I did and we arrived safely on the other side. That night at supper my father asked me if I wanted to hear a lecture on 'America at War.' I was anxious to hear it so I went to the Big Tent with my parents." After a lengthy introduction, the speaker was finally announced as "a leading candidate for the Presidency of the United States, Warren G. Harding." The youngster was properly impressed that his "new friend" was a man of such stature. Dick claims that Harding did not influence his decision, but it is interesting to note that he took up the piccolo and joined the school band the following year.

Senator Warren G. Harding. *Ohio Historical Society Archives/Library (OHS 5801).*

4

Entrepreneurial Management

As the circuit chautauqua movement rolled along, Keith Vawter's operation was the model for the entrepreneurs who followed in his footsteps. Both Roy Ellison and Charles Horner were trained under Vawter's direction on Vawter's midwestern circuit. Both left Vawter to establish their own chautauqua circuits. Harry P. Harrison, a partner of Vawter in the Redpath Bureau, followed the Vawter model when he launched the Redpath-Chicago Chautauqua circuit in 1912. In the same year Crawford A. Peffer formed the Redpath Chautauquas of New York and New England, which opened with the 1913 season.

Keith Vawter was known throughout the country as the father of circuit chautauquas. Signs outside Cedar Rapids, Iowa, where Vawter grew up, proclaimed the town as the "home of Keith Vawter, founder of the circuit chautauqua." Vawter recruited his staff of advance men and tent superintendents from ranks of younger men, turning over the active direction of each operation to the men he selected. Many businessmen and administrators attributed their success to the experience they gained in managing one of Vawter's chautauqua units.

Keith Vawter had been born in Indianola, Iowa, and attended Drake University. As a young man in his twenties, he was associated with the bookselling firm of Vawter and Son in Des Moines. In 1899 he founded the Standard Lecture Bureau, and three years later he became affiliated with the Redpath Lyceum Bureau in Chicago. A year later he organized the Redpath Chautauquas, Inc.

Harry P. Harrison, front left, one of circuit chautauqua's pioneers and a partner of Keith Vawter in the expanding chautauqua movement. *Redpath Chautauqua Collection, Special Collections Department, University of Iowa Libraries, Iowa City, Iowa.*

Meeting of chautauqua superintendents; standing, second from left, is Eben Schultz, and seated, third from left, is Richie Schultz. *Schultz Family Chautauqua Collection.*

Both Richie and Eben Schultz were among the beneficiaries of Vawter's training. As the on-site representatives of chautauqua's top management, the superintendents played a crucial role, honing their skills in public relations, marketing, personnel, and financial controls in the process. Keith Vawter valued the contribution of the bright young men he hired as superintendents and made sure that they knew they were appreciated. Outlining plans for the 1922 season, Vawter wrote that he was assigning "three of the best men that ever graced the platform" to function as superintendents in Iowa. The three included Richie and Eben Schultz.

Canton, Missouri, the hometown of the Schultz brothers, was proud of their success. When Eben turned up as the superintendent for the Canton chautauqua in 1921, Canton experienced one of its most exciting and successful chautauqua seasons. After Richie served as superintendent of Chautauqua Week in Geddes, North Dakota, the Canton newspaper printed an article headlined "Canton Boy Pleases":

The *Charles Mix County News* of Geddes, North Dakota, in the write-up of chautauqua at that place held a short time ago, closes with the following paragraph, which will be of interest to many Canton people: "John Richie Schultz is the manager of the Vawter Chautauqua System and he is a live wire, making many friends in his gentlemanly way of looking after the interests of his company and his painstaking desire to please our people and he is succeeding in both. We hope to have this young man with us again next season and are sure that he will receive a most hearty welcome."

In 1923 Crawford Peffer, the astute and highly regarded president of Redpath Chautauquas of New York and New England, approached Richie with an offer to join his organization. Because of Peffer's reputation, and because of a desire to explore the northeast, Richie was receptive. He signed a contract to become part of Peffer's management team in the summer of 1924. It portended well for him because he was destined to become the general superintendent of the circuit, reporting directly to Peffer.

It was a transitional year for Richie in other ways. In the fall of 1923, he took a sabbatical leave from his teaching job at Allegheny College and toured the southern states from Florida to Texas as a chautauqua superintendent. He first joined a five-day circuit that opened in Tarpon Springs, Florida, and closed in Mobile, Alabama. He then transferred to the larger seven-day circuit, which extended into Texas. Both circuits were under the direction of Harry P. Harrison, Vawter's former partner and the manager of the Redpath office in Chicago.

After completing his assignments in the south, Richie joined Peffer to open the 1924 season in Niagara Falls. In short order he was promoted to the position of general superintendent of the New York–New England circuit, replacing George Dalgety, who had resigned to take a position as assistant treasurer of his alma mater, Northwestern University. Dalgety had brought to Peffer years of experience in circuit chautauqua management from the days he had traveled with chautauquas in the Midwest. Richie's reputation had grown with his experience on Vawter's circuit, so Peffer was comfortable placing him in the general superintendent position. Richie's salary was $100 a week (a tidy sum at that time) with $25 for living expenses and an automobile allowance of $150 for the season, with Redpath paying for his gasoline and oil. In accepting his new position, Richie was committing to semiannual trips, usually to New York, to meet with Peffer and

Chautauqua Parade in Columbia, Mississippi. *Redpath Chautauqua Collection, Special Collections Department, University of Iowa Libraries, Iowa City, Iowa.*

his staff for planning purposes. Eben followed Richie to the Northeast to become a superintendent on the same circuit.

The New York–New England circuit was known for the high quality of its programming. Crawford A. Peffer, like Vawter, was a product of the lyceums. He developed a lifelong interest in lectures and other platform presentations while still a student in western Pennsylvania. At Allegheny College, from which he graduated in 1892, he attended lyceum courses that were offered by the college. During summer vacations he worked at the Chautauqua Institution, where he had the opportunity to hear and meet many notable personalities. Among them was the poet James Whitcomb Riley, who was giving public readings at the institution. One evening Peffer was sitting on the veranda of the Athanaeum Hotel when he noticed Riley being lionized by several attractive young women. Peffer heard Riley say "Please excuse me." He headed for Peffer as though he had business with him, muttering to himself, "those damn girls." He sat down with Peffer and began to talk rapidly about inconsequential things, averting the attention of the young women. Riley was one of the many celebrities Peffer met during his summers working at Chautauqua.

Peffer had been a pre-law student at Allegheny and went to Pittsburgh to pursue graduate studies in the law. To help finance his graduate program, he applied for a job with the Redpath Bureau, covering western Pennsylvania and Ohio. His interest and enthusiasm for the work was so intense that he was soon devoting more time to the booking business than to law studies. He finally gave up the pursuit of law to become manager of the Redpath Lyceum Bureau for Pennsylvania and the southern states, with his headquarters in Philadelphia. While there he auditioned and hired Ella Harding, a twenty-one-year-old soprano, to perform with a popular vocal group, the College Singing Girls. They toured under the auspices of the Redpath Bureau while Ella also sang with the New York Light Opera. Ella was a cousin of future president Warren G. Harding. In 1910 she and Crawford Peffer were married.

Meanwhile, Peffer had moved the offices of the Redpath Bureau from Philadelphia to White Plains, New York, twenty-five miles northeast of New York City. With the rising swell of popularity for tent chautauquas generated by Keith Vawter's innovative efforts in the Midwest, Peffer obtained the right to use the name "Redpath Chautauquas of New York and New England." In 1912 he formed a corporation with Keith Vawter and George Dalgety as minority stockholders. The following year Peffer launched the New York–New England circuit with Dalgety, a veteran of the Midwest chautauquas, as general superintendent.

The 1913 season began in June in Niagara Falls and closed in Waterville, Maine, in early September. It was a pattern that continued until the demise of the traveling chautauquas in 1932. The New York–New England circuit, when fully developed, consisted of seventy towns (see Appendix C). It offered an advantage over most chautauqua circuits because the climate was cooler and traveling was easier; there was an average of only thirty miles between towns.

While Crawford Peffer was launching his New York–New England circuit, another entrepreneur was establishing the Pennsylvania Chautauqua Association, later known as the Swarthmore Chautauqua. It was headed by Paul Pearson, a Quaker and Swarthmore College professor of speech, who made a name for himself as an orator on the lyceum circuit.

Crawford A. Peffer. *Chautauqua Collection, Pelletier Library, Allegheny College, Meadville, Pennsylvania.*

Sarah Tyson Rorer ~
of Ladies Home Journal Staff

The College Singing Girls

Gertrude Crosby

Ferrel Shafer

Florence Brady

Katherine La Sheck

The College Singing Girls (after Ella Harding left the cast). *Schultz Family Chautauqua Collection.*

Crawford A. Peffer in 1927. *Schultz Family Chautauqua Collection.*

Paul Pearson. *Friends Historical Library of Swarthmore College.*

Pearson combined an academic background with a flare for business. Initially, he operated two circuits, which served communities in New Jersey, Maryland, Delaware, West Virginia, Virginia, eastern Pennsylvania, and parts of New York State. His first circuit opened in Chestertown, Maryland, in June 1912, with 23 towns. The addition of a second circuit brought the number of towns to 41. Three years later, in 1915, the number of towns had grown to 250 in thirteen states. By 1921 the Swarthmore Chautauqua was serving eight hundred towns with four circuits. Swarthmore was known for its high moral tone and the intellectual quality of its talent. Paul Pearson established high standards and held to them. He was also an innovator and introduced the Junior Chautauqua concept, widely copied by other chautauqua organizations.

Vawter, Peffer, Harrison, Ellison, Horner, and Pearson were among the entrepreneurs who pioneered the tent chautauqua movement. They were sound businessmen, willing to take risks, and sensitive to the cultural needs and preferences of the communities in which they operated. Collectively, they changed the cultural map of America.

Richie Schultz (left) with members of his chautauqua crew. *Schultz Family Chautauqua Collection.*

5

Chautauqua Logistics

The first transcontinental railroad was completed in 1869, paving the way for a significant expansion of the American railroad system in the following decades. This was a boon to the traveling chautauquas, which relied on the railroads to transport much of their equipment and carry the performers from one town to another. Harry Harrison, head of the Redpath-Chicago circuit, turned to the railroads for a promotional stunt when he lined up a Redpath Chautauqua Special to carry chautauqua performers and boosters from Chicago to the opening of chautauqua in Albany, Georgia. With banners flying as the train moved through the countryside, it was so successful that Harrison arranged similar trips to other chautauqua locations.

But travel by rail had its downside. Moving each day from one town to the next was often exhausting, particularly if there was no "Chautauqua Special" and it meant getting up at four in the morning to catch the only available train. Eben Schultz recounts the story of trying to get to Fargo, North Dakota. No passenger train was available, so he obtained special permission from the Northern Pacific Railroad to ride in the caboose on one of its freight trains. He described the trip: "It was the hottest day of summer and the caboose was the hottest thing in the hottest place possible—an unending track of crushed rock and rails! . . . I had to sit sideways on a hard leather cushion, but I could see out the rear door and also command a full view of the 'house' where the trainmen slept and cooked their meals." On another occasion Eben caught a ride to Algona, Iowa, where his brother, Richie,

The Redpath Chautauqua Special. *Chautauqua Institution Archives, Chautauqua, New York.*

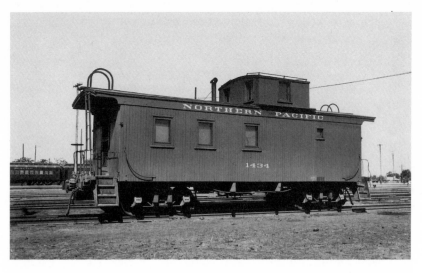

A Northern Pacific Railroad caboose. *California State Railroad Museum.*

was the superintendent of the local chautauqua. After their visit, Eben left town with Richie's crew, riding in a truck on top of the tent canvas. When crew members started singing, "I Went to the Animal Fair," Eben joined in.

The railroads failed one group of chautauqua performers in 1913, when heavy floods inundated parts of Texas. Scheduled to travel by train from Cooper to Greenville, Texas, the performers had to go miles out of their way, at times carrying heavy suitcases as they splattered through the mud. They managed to ride part of the way in a liveryman's rig and finally arrived in Greenville on a small handcar. They arrived at the chautauqua grounds ten minutes before the start of the program. The local sponsors of the Redpath-Horner Chautauqua were relieved and expressed appreciation when a bedraggled senator, scheduled for a featured lecture, handed them his unused railroad ticket. There were few chautauqua performers who did not subscribe to the adage, "the show must go on."

Travel by train was so sporadic—and sometimes not even available—that many chautauqua performers drove their own cars or hired drivers as a guarantee that they could get to the next town on time. It didn't always work. In a diary now held by Pat Kessler, Verne Jay, an actor on Vawter's seven-day circuit, described the experience of driving through the Midwest with other members of his acting troupe, traveling in a new Ford sedan and a Ford truck:

> On the whole our Fords behaved quite well on the long trek over sometimes impossible roads. However, flat tires were commonplace, and Cliff and I became expert at removing the inner tubes, repairing them, and replacing them in the tire. Once, as our truck shot over the top of a hill, a tire suddenly came off a front wheel and rolled down the hill ahead of us while Cliff brought the truck to a stop without turning into a ditch. Rain and mud were our big enemies. Several times during the season we would be unable to negotiate a hill. Then everyone got out of the cars. We unloaded them and pushed them to the top of the hill. Then we lugged our heavy suitcases from the bottom to the top of the hill.
>
> Once we traveled all day in a downpour. By late afternoon we were only a few miles from our destination. We came to a small stream and found that the bridge had been washed away. The only other bridge was nearly fifty miles away. We could have stopped at a village and notified the superintendent that we'd be unable to give the performance that night. But Toppy [the director of the troupe] was never deterred

The Pollard Players on Associated Chautauqua tour of 1926 near Pipestone, Minnesota (left to right: Marion Bronson, Cleone Pollard, and Bob Pollard). *Pat and Bill Kessler Chautauqua Collection.*

by storms. We made the nearly one-hundred-mile detour over strange, slippery roads, much of the time in darkness, and arrived at our destination about ten o'clock at night. We soon discovered that the tent had been blown down and the superintendent had acquired the use of a church. When we got there we expected to find it dark. To our amazement the church was jammed to the doors with expectant townspeople and farmers. Although we were dirty and bone-tired, we hastily set the stage and gave what was probably the best performance of the season. That evening brought home to me that chautauqua held a very unique place in the lives of these entertainment-starved people.

Verne Jay had gotten his start on chautauqua while a student at Cornell College in Iowa. He and a classmate, Cleone Harker, had teamed up to do dramatic skits while they were students in West Waterloo High School. They continued to perform in plays as a thespian duo after they both enrolled at Cornell. Their dramatic talent caught the attention of Clyde "Toppy" Tull, a producer of plays for the Redpath-Vawter Chautauqua circuit. Tull was an English professor at Cornell who toured on chautauqua with a troupe of actors during the summer months. Many of the actors were students who returned to

Bob Pollard, Marion Bronson, and Cleone Pollard, after a few thousand miles on the 1926 tour. *Pat and Bill Kessler Chautauqua Collection.*

the campus at the end of the season. Verne got his first taste of chautauqua at the end of his sophomore year, when Toppy recruited him as a midsummer replacement for an actor who had to leave the company.

In their junior year Verne and Cleone were approached by Toppy to join his acting company for the full summer season of 1923. The play was a Broadway comedy, *Adam and Eva.* They performed in 101 towns that summer, in Iowa, Minnesota, North and South Dakota, Nebraska, and Montana. By the end of the season, they were exhausted from seven thousand miles of grueling travel, most of it over unimproved dirt roads. As Cleone's daughter later remarked, it was "a killer schedule," but Cleone was undeterred. She accepted the vicissitudes of the vagabond life and was eager to embark on another season.

The following year she joined Verne, who, with Toppy's support, had formed his own company, the Verne Jay Players. Verne and Toppy took it on the Redpath-Vawter Chautauqua circuit, starting in upper Minnesota on June 4 and closing the season in Denton, Kansas, on September 4. Bob Pollard, another Cornell College graduate, was also in the cast. Before the season was over, he and Cleone were mar-

"No filling station in sight": Bob Pollard in northern South Dakota, June 1926. *Pat and Bill Kessler Chautauqua Collection.*

ried. Seizing the opportunity to pursue a professional career in the theater, they formed the Pollard Players and toured on chautauqua until its waning days.

With their own company, the Pollards continued to crisscross the country, traveling by car over treacherous roads to fulfill the demands of a merciless schedule. Their contract with Associated Chautauquas of America in 1927 called for them to perform in 111 towns in twenty-one states in a four-month period (see Appendix D).

The Associated Chautauquas system formed after World War I through the acquisition of a number of small circuits in various parts of the country. The Pollards persevered and even thrived on the nomadic life. As a child, their daughter, Pat, traveled with her parents and has "vivid memories" of those days:

> They would always write in a small part, usually just a line or two, for me; and of course, it was thrilling and such fun to step out on that stage! I can remember the big canvas tents and the rows of folding chairs or uncomfortable benches lined up for the audience. It could be mighty hot under the tent, but no one seemed to mind too much.

THE POLLARD PLAYERS

Wish Success to All for the Coming Season

BOB and CLEONE POLLARD

Presenting "LAFF THAT OFF" With Federated Bureaus This Winter

AVAILABLE NOW FOR
1930 AND 1931

PAST FOUR SEASONS
WITH ASSOCIATED

Bob and Cleone Pollard. *Pat and Bill Kessler Chautauqua Collection.*

The fascinating thing for me was my Dad's makeup kit, with its fake hair and spirit gum for applying beards and eyebrows, plus tubes and tubes of greasepaint. I loved to watch him transform himself into a crusty old man.

After the circuit chautauquas folded their tents and faded away in the early 1930s, the Pollard Players continued to perform on the lyceum stage. Later, Bob Pollard starred in many radio dramas and stage plays.

Singer and actress Louise Day traveled on the Ellison-White circuit as a member of the Winters Trio. She wrote of her experience:

> Most of our traveling was done by train and it was rough going. We were shaken apart by poor roadbeds and covered with soot and cinders from the engine's soft coal. With few exceptions the hotels were poor and the food bad. As we crossed over into Canada, some of the jumps between towns had to be made by car because there were no railroads.
>
> Our final jump was from Twin Bridges, Montana, to Salmon, Idaho. Salmon was to be our last stop and we almost never made it. That eleven-hour trip was a veritable nightmare. Our driver was drunk. He got lost, skidded around hairpin turns over wild mountainous terrain at a terrifying speed, and once narrowly escaped plunging over a precipice into a deep ravine. It's a wonder we ever arrived, and when we did, we were all badly shaken. There was barely time to make the afternoon performance. The tent was jammed with people patiently awaiting our arrival.

Having survived the frightening drive, the Winters Trio was confronted with an even greater hazard. As Louise continues the story:

> Just as we were about to start the show, a huge cloud enveloped us. A fierce wind shook the tent, tugging at the ropes, and the air was tinged with a menacing yellow hue. A full-fledged Idaho dust storm was bearing down upon us in all its fury. Tent sides flapped wildly and the poles swayed back and forth as if they would break any minute.
>
> Ted Winters rushed out on the stage and yelled, "Everybody go home! No performance this afternoon—GO HOME!" Nobody moved. One man in overalls stood up and shouted, "We git plenty o' these storms. We ain't scared." Ted shouted back, "Maybe you ain't, but we are." With that, and with stinging dust in our eyes, face, and throat, Carol and I made a dash through the dressing tent into the open air. Ted was just behind us when the small tent's supporting pole gave way.

Storm-damaged tent. *Schultz Family Chautauqua Collection.*

A flying splinter struck him on the right temple and he fell to the ground unconscious. Carol dragged him outside and I screamed for a doctor.

All of a sudden the storm was over as quickly as it had come. Miraculously the main tent, which had been straining at the ropes like some enormous, tethered monster, still stood. The doctor had dressed Ted's wounds and he soon regained consciousness. He said he felt fine and brusquely ordered us to get ready for the evening show.

We had a capacity audience that night. A hush fell over the crowd and tension mounted as the people watched Ted asking me to sing. As the last notes of my song died away, Ted Winters slumped in his chair, his cane clattering to the floor. There was no laughter this time — only silence. Ted had at last achieved his dream of a perfect performance but was not there to know it. My chautauqua career ended on this tragic note.

Wave Noggle, a resident of Normal, Illinois, was a crew member on Redpath Chautauqua's midwestern circuit during the summers of

The threat of storms did not dampen the enthusiasm for chautauqua. *Schultz Family Chautauqua Collection.*

1926 and 1927. "That was one of the ways I made my way through college," he explained. At the time, he was a student at Illinois State Normal University, now Illinois State University. The job not only helped pay his college expenses but also provided the opportunity for him to enjoy the chautauqua attractions. Mr. Noggle recalled

> the interesting variety of programs on the chautauqua schedule. There was A. I. Root and his lecture-demonstrations with two swarms of bees. There was a beautiful production of the opera *Madame Butterfly,* and lectures by the daughter of William Jennings Bryan, Ruth Bryan Owen. In 1925, the summer before I joined the circuit, John Philip Sousa's band was a big attraction.
>
> There was a big pup tent in the back of the main tent where we slept. We traveled from town to town in a rented baggage car. All the equipment—the canvas tent, tent poles, stakes, ropes, and folding chairs—all went into the baggage car. We had cots for sleeping in the baggage car, too. Our circuit extended from Georgia, Florida, the Carolinas, Tennessee, and Kentucky in the south to Michigan, Indiana, and Illinois in the north.

It wasn't only the movement of people and equipment that challenged chautauqua officials, but also the difficulty in providing creature comforts for the performers in small towns unaccustomed to hosting people of prominence. The greasy foods in local restaurants could be awful, and chautauqua performers, particularly on the midwestern circuits, complained of an overdose of fried chicken. Eben called Richmond, Missouri, the "Fried-Chicken Center of America." In the dining room of his hotel in Richmond, fried chicken, piled high on platters, was served family style for breakfast, dinner (in small-town America, "dinner" often refers to the midday meal), and supper. Fortunately there were occasional invitations to dine with local officials

PROPERTY OF JOHN J. BUSE HISTORICAL MUSEUM

Chautauqua had a strong presence throughout the Midwest, where it drew this opening audience in St. Charles, Missouri, ca. 1914. *John J. Buse Jr. Collection, 1860–1931, Western Historical Manuscript Collection–Columbia, Missouri.*

who outdid themselves to provide a spread of tasty home-cooked specialties. When chautauqua played in Canton, Missouri, as it did every summer, Laura Schultz, mother of the two Schultz brothers, always put on a big spread for the chautauqua staff and performers.

The local chautauqua committees were crucial to the success of chautauqua. They facilitated the advance sale of tickets and provided the guarantees that chautauquas required. As much as small communities might welcome the cultural advantages of chautauqua, it was often a struggle for them to meet the guarantee. Ruby Aldinger, a retired public health nurse, remembers chautauqua coming to her hometown of Turtle Lake, North Dakota, and pitching the tent just two blocks from her home. Etched in her memory was her father's concern that Turtle Lake, a small town with a population of only 680 people, might not fulfill its quota of advance ticket sales. As the owner of a cream station and one of the town's leading citizens, he was one of the guarantors. It was a risk he took in the interests of the community. To the credit of Mr. Aldinger and the other guarantors, all of the required tickets were sold, enabling them to support the same full week of chautauqua programs experienced by much larger communities.

In Butler, Pennsylvania, a manufacturing town of fifteen thousand people, the Chamber of Commerce played a pivotal role in bringing chautauqua to town for the first time. The success of the chamber's efforts prompted the *Butler Citizen* to publish an editorial extolling the merits of chautauqua:

> When the subject of an outdoor chautauqua for Butler was broached last spring and a preliminary canvass was made, there were many who felt little interest in the subject, and there were others who were certain that such a thing would not be a success in this city. If there are any who are still lacking interest in the work of the Redpath Chautauqua, they are not among those who attended the sessions throughout last week, and if there are any who still feel that it could not be made a success in Butler, they have not informed themselves on the large and enthusiastic crowds which were in daily attendance.
> The people of Butler and vicinity owe a debt of gratitude to the Chamber of Commerce and to the active committee of that body which worked so faithfully and zealously, assuming financial risk in order that

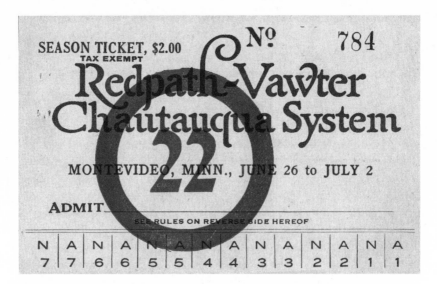

Season ticket, Montevideo, Minnesota, chautauqua 1922. *Chautauqua Collection, Pelletier Library, Allegheny College, Meadville, Pennsylvania.*

the chautauqua might be brought to Butler. Thanks are also due to others who assisted in the work of securing the greatest possible patronage for the chautauqua this year and insuring its return for another season. The Redpath system enables communities like Butler to secure talent of a high order at a minimum of cost to the individual. The advance sale of tickets secures a guarantee of actual expenses, and the chautauqua management takes the risk of getting its profit out of the sale of single admissions. This first year there were 1,174 adult season tickets sold, and it is believed that the single admission sales were large enough to secure to Butler the reputation of being one of the desirable chautauqua stations.

In subsequent years the town of Butler became a regular stop on the Redpath-Brockway Chautauqua circuit. The inaugural season in 1913 introduced local residents to the Ben Greet Players, who put on a production of Oliver Goldsmith's *She Stoops to Conquer.* Also on the program were Bohumir Kryl and his concert band and orator Joseph W. Folk, former governor of Missouri. A highlight of the week was a debate on the merits of socialism between Adam Bede, a Republican congressman from Minnesota for eight years, and Emil Seidel, mayor of Milwaukee, who had been elected in 1910 on the Socialist ticket. Bede and Seidel teamed up to tour on the summer chautauquas to take advantage of a growing interest in the issue of socialism versus capitalism.

Chautauqua first came to Oneida, New York, in 1914, with a six-day program that started on August 28 and closed on September 3. Chautauqua's debut in Oneida was accompanied by all of the fanfare that other chautauqua communities had already experienced. Flags and banners announcing chautauqua flew from every pole in town, and a band greeted the performers on arrival. The chautauqua caravan moved through the town to vacant property on Cemetery Street behind the Elizabeth Street School. It was there that the giant tent was raised. The initial program included a performance of Shakespeare's *The Taming of the Shrew* by the Ben Greet Players, whom Crawford Peffer had booked for Redpath just the year before. It was a rare opportunity for local residents to witness a live stage presentation by one of the most illustrious ensembles of Shakespearian actors in the world.

The success of the first Oneida chautauqua can be measured by the response of the community, which renewed the chautauqua contract

THE BEN GREET PLAYERS AT CHANCELLOR HOUSE, TUNBRIDGE WELLS.

from Philip Ben Greet

"Because their business still lies out o' door."

"Comedy of Errors."

The Ben Greet Players. *Chautauqua Collection, Pelletier Library, Allegheny College, Meadville, Pennsylvania.*

every year through 1932. In an editorial, the *Oneida Dispatch* marveled at the precision and competence of the chautauqua organization:

> That the Chautauqua, now in operation in thousands of American cities, is one of the most marvelously organized systems under the sun is evidenced by a look at the complicated program of details that must be carried out before canvas is folded on the last day of the seven-day series of entertainments.
>
> The Chautauqua moves from town to town, from city to city, and from state to state without mishap, friction, or noise. To follow the path of the Redpath Chautauquas from the time winter quarters are abandoned and until the season closes on the lakes would furnish new ideas even to some of the greatest master organizers. No army, though backed by a government, ever moved with more graceful ease.

Despite the extravagant language, the newspaper had a point. There were sometimes glitches, but by and large the job of planning the schedule, recruiting the talent, managing the logistics, financing the programs, and promoting the performances was smoothly executed. It was a team effort, starting with the twenty-one-day and nine-day advance men and culminating with the arrival of the superintendent with his tent crew, staff, and cast of performers.

The success of chautauqua in places like Butler, Oneida, and elsewhere reflected the remarkable organization skills of a masterful team of chautauqua entrepreneurs.

Promoting chautauqua in Portsmouth, New Hampshire. *Chautauqua Collection, Pelletier Library, Allegheny College, Meadville, Pennsylvania.*

6

Chautauqua Talent — the Speechmakers

With their deep roots in the lyceum business, circuit chautauquas were able to tap into a pool of exceptional talent. The biggest names on the lecture and entertainment circuits were booked through lyceum bureaus, foremost of which was Redpath. As the tent chautauqua movement spread across the country, it expanded the opportunities available to the professional speakers, musicians, actors, and other performers who derived at least a portion of their incomes from platform presentations.

In the early days of chautauqua, programs were focused exclusively on lectures and recitations. Chautauqua audiences expected to hear rousing speeches on the political and social issues of the day or inspirational talks by noted theologians and philosophers. William Jennings Bryan, the greatest orator of his day, was a frequent chautauqua speaker. His speech "The Prince of Peace" drew record crowds.

Bryan burst onto the political scene at age thirty-six when he rallied Democrats to oppose the gold standard that was being advocated by another Democrat, the incumbent Grover Cleveland. At the party's convention in 1896, his "Cross of Gold" speech was so stirring that he defeated Cleveland and was nominated for president on the Democratic ticket. He continued to fire up audiences across the country as the Democratic candidate running against gold advocate William McKinley, the Republican candidate. Bryan lost the election but established his reputation as the nation's best-known and most sought

Left to right: Keith Vawter, William Jennings Bryan, and Bohumir Kryl.
Redpath Chautauqua Collection, Special Collections Department, University of Iowa
Libraries, Iowa City, Iowa.

after orator. His appearance on the Chautauqua platform was a guarantee of a packed house.

Rivaling William Jennings Bryan in popularity but not in oratorical style was the Reverend Russell H. Conwell, who delivered a message that townspeople loved to hear. His "Acres of Diamonds" speech exhorted audiences to look for wealth and fortune in their own backyards. There was nothing wrong, he contended, in seeking riches as long as you followed Christian precepts in the quest. There was an evangelistic fervor to his delivery, which resonated with community leaders who were disturbed that too many young men were leaving to seek their fortunes elsewhere. Conwell repeated his lecture thousands of times, season after season, in the same small towns, where summer audiences crowded into the big, hot tents to be reassured that it was all right to be rich.

When audiences approved of a speaker, they showed their appreciation by waving their handkerchiefs. This form of tribute was known as the "chautauqua salute," and receiving a sustained one assured a

Russell H. Conwell. *Redpath Chautauqua Collection, Special Collections Department, University of Iowa Libraries, Iowa City, Iowa.*

speaker that he or she would be invited back for the next season. Chautauqua salutes continued to be used until medical practitioners railed against the practice as unsanitary. No matter how they showed their appreciation, chautauqua crowds welcomed the opportunity to hear the same speech the following year, just as they would enjoy a favorite song repeated by a leading prima donna.

Because of his popularity with the crowds, the Reverend Frank Wakely Gunsaulus was always assured of a chautauqua salute. In the *American Magazine*, Keith Vawter was quoted as saying "the ideal entertainer, from our point of view, is the man whom the people like, both when they hear him speak and when they meet him on the street. Such a man, for instance, is Doctor Gunsaulus, famous Chicago minister. Doctor Gunsaulus is at heart a big, rollicking boy, and I believe it is his natural ebullience of spirit that has for these many years made him so notably successful in the pulpit." For twenty years Dr. Gunsaulus was pastor of Central Church, one of Chicago's largest, but he was equally well known as the president of Armour Institute, which he founded with the backing of the wealthy industrialist Philip D. Armour.

From the political arena, William Howard Taft, Warren G. Harding, and Robert La Follette were among the prominent speakers who brought their stories of reform and discussed the issues of the day. Joseph W. Folk, who served as governor of Missouri from 1905 to 1909, had built his reputation as an attorney by exposing corruption and prosecuting bribery cases. Chautauqua audiences responded

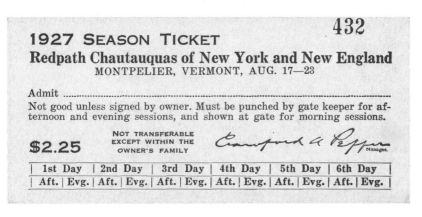

Chautauqua Collection, Pelletier Library, Allegheny College, Meadville, Pennsylvania.

to his forthright appeals for reform. Another reformer was Francis Joseph Heney of California, who argued land-grant cases before the Supreme Court and prosecuted land-fraud offenders. All of these speakers were masters of oratory, and they provided an insider's view of the political scene.

Not only Dr. Gunsaulus, but also evangelist Billy Sunday and the Reverends Cadman and Sockman left their pulpits to bring messages of spirituality to the people. The Reverend Samuel Parkes Cadman, born in England of Scottish ancestry, was the first person in America to use the medium of radio to broadcast a religious program coast to coast. The pastor of Central Congregational Church in Brooklyn, he became widely known and sought after for chautauqua engagements. He was so revered by the community of Brooklyn that Cadman Plaza, in the heart of Brooklyn's Historic District, still bears his name.

As America's best-known evangelist, Billy Sunday conducted revival meetings for throngs of people looking for spiritual guidance. In his prime from 1904 to 1907, he received from one thousand to five thousand converts a month. That didn't leave much time for other engagements, but he managed to accept occasional invitations to speak on the touring chautauquas. An ordained Presbyterian minister, a staunch Prohibitionist, and a former professional baseball player (from 1883 to 1890 he had played for the Chicago, Pittsburgh, and Philadelphia teams of the National League), Sunday added luster to any program where he was featured.

Even though chautauqua audiences were predominantly Christian, a number of prominent rabbis were booked for platform engagements. Widely known for his oratory, Rabbi Emil Gustav Kirsch was among them. Rabbi Kirsch was a reform advocate with strong and independent views on such subjects as Zionism, which he vigorously opposed. He held a post at the University of Chicago as professor of rabbinical literature and philosophy and was the author of many books and articles on biblical and other religious subjects.

Although many of the programs were entertaining, the purpose was not entertainment. They were intended to convey a serious message. In 1931 when chautauqua came to Oneida, New York, the Reverend Ralph Sockman, a renowned radio preacher and president of the New York Federation of Churches, was a featured speaker on the subject of "Gentlemen and Gangsters." With reference to his lecture he

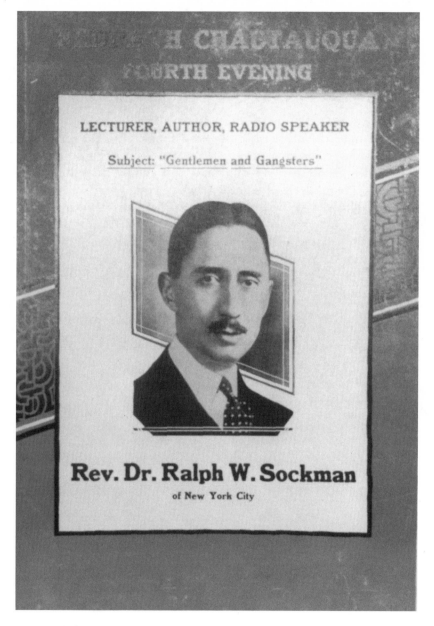

Rev. Dr. Ralph W. Sockman. *Chautauqua Collection, Pelletier Library, Allegheny College, Meadville, Pennsylvania.*

commented: "Under the cover of orderly society in America there has grown up an invisible government by gangsters. It is a rule by force and intimidation. This principle of racketeering which thrives most luxuriantly in the cities reaches out to almost every village and industry." Dr. Sockman was the charismatic minister of Madison Avenue Methodist Episcopal Church in New York City. He had a national following because of his radio broadcasts and his guest appearances in such pulpits as New York's Riverside Church. He was always a big hit with chautauqua audiences.

Even the recitations of such famous elocutionists as Katharine Ridgeway were selected to be elevating. Because there were moralistic and religious overtones to much of the programming, the local clergy became big boosters of chautauqua and often urged their parishioners to attend. Chautauqua management went out of its way to make sure that chautauqua would not be perceived by the local clergy as in any way competitive. Some chautauqua circuits held ecumenical services on Sunday evenings, encouraging participation from the various faiths of the town, but chautauqua superintendents never scheduled events on Sunday mornings.

Donald L. Graham, a chautauqua scholar at the University of Iowa, wrote in May 1952, "Chautauqua was scrupulous in its effort to maintain a high standard of decency in its programs. . . . At one time, . . . Vawter rejected a play which bordered too much on the divorce question. Speakers were asked to deposit copies of their lectures in advance with the bureau headquarters and to avoid deviation from it lest they offend by some chance statement."

The Loar-Shaw Chautauqua circuit, operating from headquarters in Bloomington, Illinois, issued guidelines for the conduct of its performances. Among them: "Sunday programs must be 'suitable'; personal conduct of performers must be above public and private criticism; and no cheap jazz music in any form."

As the prominent daughter of William Jennings Bryan, Ruth Bryan Owen drew large crowds in her own right on the chautauqua circuit. Her background as an author, educator, world traveler, and nurse in Egypt during World War I qualified her as one of chautauqua's most interesting speakers. After her husband's death in 1910, she became an advocate for women in politics and served as a member of the U.S. Congress from 1929 to 1933. She was the first woman sent to Congress by Florida, and she became a member of the important Foreign Relations Committee. At the end of her term, she was appointed by President Franklin D. Roosevelt as U.S. minister to Denmark. While serving in that capacity, she married a captain of the Danish Royal Guards. Prior to her death in 1954, she was awarded the Distinguished Service Medal by King Frederick of Denmark.

In 1928, Ruth Bryan Owen had been elected to Congress as a representative from Florida, adding to her prominence. The following year she appeared on the chautauqua platform in Niagara Falls to deliver a talk, "Opening Doors." Her speech reflected her concern, as the mother of four children, for the youth of America:

> I would like to see each of our counties select one boy and one girl as the most promising young citizens in the county. Then I would like to take these young people to Washington. I would like for them to read the Declaration of Independence in the original in its gold case in the Congressional Library, and then go to Mt. Vernon and walk in the footsteps of Washington. I would like for them to see the Supreme Court in session; to meet our President; to see the great dome of the Capitol against the sky, with the meeting of the Senate in one wing of that great building and the United States Congress in the other wing.
>
> And then I would like those young people, after a week of study of government there at the very fountain head of it to come back to their counties and report to their schools and their local groups what a wonderful thing the government of a republic really is. I would like them to see the responsibilities of a government resting equally on every citizen. I would like them to realize that we can't have one hundred percent America when only forty-six percent take the trouble to vote. And I believe that the idealism of youth would be stirred by the picture of a republic and that we would have in our district the fine enthusiasm of our young people directed toward real American citizenship.

Because of her charm and her intimate knowledge of government affairs, Mrs. Owen continued to be in demand on chautauqua circuits. Her topic in 1923, as she toured on Vawter's midwestern circuit, was "Modern Arabian Knights." During an afternoon break from her lecture schedule in Lancaster, Missouri, she and Superintendent Eben Schultz were strolling near the chautauqua tent when they spied a tree full of ripe peaches. The peaches were temptingly delicious so they reached across a sagging fence to sample them. At that point the fence gave way and guilt-ridden they scurried away, to quote Eben, "like pranksters at Halloween."

Ruth Bryan Owen. *Redpath Chautauqua Collection, Special Collections Department, University of Iowa Libraries, Iowa City, Iowa.*

Mabel Walker Willebrandt. *Redpath Chautauqua Collection, Special Collections Department, University of Iowa Libraries, Iowa City, Iowa.*

Another featured speaker on the New York–New England circuit was a brilliant lawyer, Mabel Walker Willebrandt, who at a 1925 chautauqua assembly gave a speech entitled "Courts, Crooks, and the Constitution." Her reputation as a powerful attorney in California catapulted her into the national spotlight and led to her appointment as assistant attorney general of the United States, a post she held from 1921 to 1929. On a subsequent chautauqua tour, she lectured on the importance of patriotic service, a subject very dear to her heart. As a Washington insider, Mrs. Willebrandt was able to offer an insightful perspective on the political scene. She was in great demand but because of a busy schedule was forced to limit her chautauqua engagements. In 1930 when she lectured in Oneida, New York, her appearance was publicized as a rare opportunity for local residents. Mrs.

Willebrandt was recognized, along with Ruth Bryan Owen and Ida Tarbell, as one of the most dynamic women in public life.

Ida M. Tarbell, the Lincoln biographer and muckraker whose book *The History of the Standard Oil Company* contributed to the breakup of the Standard Oil monopoly, was an ardent booster of chautauqua. Tarbell had grown up attending the summer sessions of the Chautauqua Institution with her parents. Later she served as editor of the institution's monthly publication, the *Chautauquan.* It was published in Meadville, Pennsylvania, about sixty miles from the institution's western New York headquarters. Tarbell was at home in Meadville, where she had resided while attending Allegheny College. She succumbed to the lure of the traveling chautauquas when she was approached by the director of a lecture bureau. She inevitably appeared as a regular speaker on the chautauqua platform. In 1920 she described the social benefits of chautauqua:

> One of the best institutions in this country is the chautauqua summer platform. Certainly in the stress of these times it should be preserved if any institution is to be preserved. . . . It brings a fresh element into the social life of the town — a very desirable thing, particularly in the smaller community. It provides stimulating ideas that the country must understand and study. Every thing now depends upon the country keeping its mind steady and active and inspiring people to full cooperation. The chautauqua platform will do this in a wonderfully direct way. Every community should be willing to sacrifice, if necessary, to keep chautauqua alive in the community.

Having never lectured before, Tarbell signed a chautauqua contract with some misgivings prior to the outbreak of World War I. It was a seven-week commitment that called for her to speak in forty-nine different places in forty-nine days. Demanding as it was, life on the traveling chautauqua circuit held a fascination for her, which she describes in her autobiographical book, *All in a Day's Work:*

> To my surprise I found myself deeply interested in the physical life of the circuit, so like the life of the circus. We performed in tents, and our outfit was as gay as ever you saw — khaki tents bound in red, with a great khaki fence about, pennants floating up and down the streets, and within, order, cleanliness, and the smartest kind of little platform and side dressing rooms.

Ida M. Tarbell at work. *Ida M. Tarbell Collection, Pelletier Library, Allegheny College, Meadville, Pennsylvania.*

Naturally I had no little curiosity about my traveling companions. Scoffing eastern friends told me that there would be bell ringers, trained dogs, and Tyrolese yodelers. I found no such entertainment, but I could hardly have fallen in with pleasanter company. I saw at once that what I had joined was not, as I had hastily imagined, a haphazard semi-business, semi-philanthropic, happy-go-lucky new kind of barnstorming. It was serious business.

The chautauqua management was much more professional than she had expected. In truth, bell ringers, trained dogs, and yodelers were sometimes a feature of chautauqua programs, primarily those for children, but they were subordinate to the main attractions—orators like William Jennings Bryan, public figures like Warren Harding, and journalists of note like Tarbell herself. In 1919, at the conclusion of World War I, Tarbell distinguished herself by lecturing again on the chautauqua platform following the signing of the Treaty of Versailles at the Paris Peace Conference. Her topic was "The U.S. at the Peace

Conference." She was the editor of *McClure's Magazine,* and her views were widely respected.

Interest in the war and postwar society continued to be reflected in chautauqua programming into the 1920s. During the war, President Woodrow Wilson had labeled chautauqua "an integral part of the national defense" because of its wholesome entertainment, stirring music, and contribution to keeping up the morale of the armed forces. Theodore Roosevelt called it "the most American thing in America." Other prominent leaders in American life who attended its sessions or spoke from its platform added their tributes.

D. Thomas Curtin, world famous as an American journalist and author, saw fighting on eighteen fronts during World War I as a war correspondent for the *London Times,* the *London Daily Mail,* and a syndicate of American newspapers. At various times he was attached to the Austrian, German, Russian, Romanian, Serbian, Italian, French, British, and American armies. He toured with the Redpath chautauquas in 1923 to deliver a lecture, "What's the Matter with Europe," in which he discussed social and economic conditions in Europe and how they affected the rest of the world.

Drew Pearson, who later gained prominence as a newspaper correspondent and columnist ("Washington Merry-Go-Round"), began his career on the Swarthmore Chautauqua circuit. As the fourteen-year-old son of the founder, Drew traveled on the first year of the circuit as a member of the three-man tent crew. He recalled the experience:

> I remember vividly going to a town called Shenandoah, Pennsylvania, deep in the anthracite coal belt. The population of Shenandoah was 30,000, of which less than 50% could speak English. When we opened there, they had to call out the National Guard to protect us, not physically, but because the people were curious and didn't have any money. They came up and slashed our tent sidewall. We just had to have help. Our entertainment was like a breath of revolution. They'd never seen anything like it before. On the whole they didn't care much for the lectures. Then, as the years went on, they did, but that first year was really rough going, as far as lectures were concerned. Much of it was over their heads. My salary when I started out was $12 a week, and in the fall I got $14 a week. The next spring I got $16 a week.

By 1918 at age twenty, Drew Pearson was working as a platform superintendent on the Ellison-White Chautauqua circuit and earning

D. THOMAS CURTIN

Schultz Family Chautauqua Collection.

fifty dollars a week. Pearson described his living conditions as a crew member:

> We slept in the tents. We had a pup tent behind and we brought in water. We carried water from where we'd get it, and we had basins in which we took a splash bath. Once in awhile we'd find a river or someplace we could get in a swim.

Unloading stage props for a chautauqua performance. *Chautauqua Collection, Pelletier Library, Allegheny College, Meadville, Pennsylvania.*

One of the places I remember was Bel Air, Maryland, where [William Jennings] Bryan spoke. I had been on the tent crew and I was in charge of the platform. My job was to see that the lights were on, the steps were in good order, and the proper things on the platform. We didn't have microphones, and we didn't have rostrums. We had a plain, flat kitchen table. For most of the talent I had a bucket and a dipper to one side—but not the audience side—but for Bryan [who was secretary of state at the time] I always borrowed a pitcher.

Pearson also commented on Bryan's booming voice: "There were no microphones, but he didn't need one."

Drew Pearson reappeared on the platform of the Swarthmore Chautauqua circuit in 1921 to deliver an illustrated lecture, "The New Power in Southern Europe." He had just returned from a two-year assignment in Europe where he was engaged in relief work for post-war Serbia under the auspices of the Friends Reconstruction Service. Having traveled extensively through the Balkans in the course of his work, he was able to provide a firsthand account of conditions in Albania, Austria, Greece, Hungary, Italy, Turkey, and Yugoslavia. Young

Schultz Family Chautauqua Collection.

Pearson, like his father, was a gifted speaker, as well as a writer, and became a headliner on many lyceum and chautauqua programs.

On the same bill with Drew Pearson during the 1921 summer season was Dr. Gregory Zilboorg, a revolutionary and former member of the Russian cabinet. Dr. Zilboorg served as undersecretary of labor during the short administration of Aleksandr Kerensky, who became premier after the monarchy was abolished in 1917 and Czar Nicholas was forced to abdicate. Kerensky himself was overthrown by Bolshevik forces led by Lenin in November 1917. Resorting to a number of ruses, Dr. Zilboorg had escaped and made his way to America. The Russian Revolution was a topic of intense interest to Americans and was a surefire hit on the chautauqua circuits.

The year 1921 marked the tenth anniversary of the Swarthmore Chautauqua, and Paul Pearson had lined up an exceptional array of talent for the occasion. In addition to Dr. Zilboorg and Drew Pearson, the program included Dr. Frank Bohn, a well-known orator, historian, and writer for the *New York Times,* who also spoke about economic and social conditions in both Europe and America. Elliott A. Boyl, an inspirational speaker, added a note of compassion with his talk, "The Advantage of a Handicap." The week also included performances by a

Dr. Gregory Zilboorg. *Friends Historical Library of Swarthmore College.*

Russian band, a string quartet, and a light opera company that staged *The Bohemian Girl.*

Because of chautauqua's popularity and the exposure it gave people of prominence, particularly politicians, chautauqua management had little difficulty in lining up quality talent. But negotiating contracts wasn't always easy. Crawford Peffer told the story of negotiating with former U.S. president Howard Taft for a chautauqua engagement. He described the arrangements and mentioned the salary he was prepared to pay. "Oh, the salary is all right," grinned the ex-president. "What kind of grub do they have out there?"

On a similar mission, Peffer went to see Warren G. Harding, then a senator. Senator Walter S. Kenyon of Iowa had been secured for half the season. It was all the time Kenyon could give, so he suggested that Peffer approach Harding for the other half. Harding agreed, then asked, "How about the salary?"

"Six hundred dollars a week," replied Peffer.

"I don't know that that's enough," said Harding.

"Kenyon took it," said Peffer.

Harding retorted, "But I'll make you a much better speech than Kenyon." In telling the story, Peffer acknowledged that he did.

Robert A. McCown, manuscripts librarian at the University of Iowa, in an article he wrote for the *Henry Ford Museum and Greenfield Village Herald,* tells the story of Senator Robert M. La Follette of Wisconsin, a popular headliner on the chautauqua circuits. One of La Follette's favorite topics was "special privilege," and he was known for giving the audience its money's worth. One chautauqua superintendent, when asked what "Fighting Bob" talked about, said, "about four hours. The first two hours the farmers in the audience wanted to rush to Washington and shoot Speaker Joe Cannon. After that they were for Cannon and wanted to shoot La Follette."

Chautauqua became an influential voice for advocates of alcohol prohibition. Governor Frank Hanly of Indiana was a tireless spokesman for Prohibition on chautauqua circuits and in 1916 was nominated for president by the Prohibition Party. In the summer of 1916, Governor Malcolm R. Patterson of Tennessee toured on a chautauqua circuit to deliver a lecture on "the liquor problem." In 1918 the International Lyceum and Chautauqua Association passed a resolution in support of Prohibition.

Robert M. La Follette. *State Historical Society of Wisconsin WHi (X3) 45820.*

Women's Christian Temperance Union tent at the Racine Chautauqua, 1906. *State Historical Society of Wisconsin WHi (B531) 344.*

The evangelist Billy Sunday, in his occasional appearances on chautauqua, spoke out against the pitfalls of alcoholism and on the need to strengthen the moral fabric of America. But the most vocal of the temperance activists was Carrie Nation, who smashed bottles in saloons with a hatchet and carried her message to the chautauqua stage, often passing out miniature hatchets to the audience. Colorful and controversial, she was a popular speaker on some of the smaller chautauqua circuits, but she was never booked by the more conservative Redpath chautauquas.

Women's suffrage was another issue that appealed to chautauqua communities. Jane Addams of Chicago's Hull House was a leading advocate of women's voting rights. She was well known as a pioneer for social justice and the founder of Hull House, a social settlement on Chicago's West Side. She was actively involved in the peace

Jane Addams (center) and Bishop Vincent (left), the cofounder of the Chautauqua Institution. *Jane Addams Memorial Collection (JAMC neg. 49), The University Library, University of Illinois at Chicago.*

movement in the early part of the twentieth century and in 1931 was awarded the Nobel Peace Prize. As a forceful voice for suffrage, she made occasional speeches from the chautauqua platform, while some of her disciples became regulars on the chautauqua circuits.

Jeannette Rankin, the first woman to be elected to the House of Representatives, was another suffragette who railed against the injustice of a political system in which half of society was disenfranchised. It had been a long journey from the Montana ranch where she was born to the halls of Congress in 1917. As the first woman elected to Congress, she acquired a national forum to continue her work on behalf of women's suffrage. To strengthen her credibility as an advocate for women's rights, she had worked as a seamstress to gain personal knowledge of social conditions. Chautauqua gave her the exposure she needed to drive home her passionate message.

Social issues were addressed on the chautauqua platform by advocates of women's suffrage and prohibition, but circuit chautauqua was noticeably silent on the plight of African Americans. At the same time, African American activists were aggressively pursuing a civil rights agenda. Their views were articulated most forcibly by W. E. B. Du Bois, a prominent educator and author, and Marcus Garvey, who headed a nationalist movement advocating a return to Africa for African Americans, with the promise of a utopian freedom from persecution and discrimination. The fact that Du Bois, Garvey, and others who shared what many at that time considered to be radical views, did not speak from the chautauqua stage is not surprising. Keith Vawter was on record as favoring a middle-of-the road approach, avoiding programs that might be too controversial to be accepted by the typically conservative patrons. There was a level of tolerance beyond which chautauqua audiences and their sponsors were not willing to go. Chautauqua management always had its eye on the financial guarantees of the local sponsors, who had to be satisfied if a contract was to be signed for the following year.

Yet African American entertainers were another matter. The many religious singing groups always received a warm welcome on the chautauqua circuits. The Fisk Jubilee Singers from Fisk University was one of the most popular. So were other African American musicians, both soloists and instrumental groups.

A few black lecturers toured on chautauqua, but it was understood by contractual arrangement that they would stay clear of controversial

The Fisk Jubilee Singers—popular chautauqua entertainers. *Redpath Chautauqua Collection, Special Collections Department, University of Iowa Libraries, Iowa City, Iowa.*

subjects. Professor Laurence C. Jones, founder of the Piney Woods Country Life School in Mississippi, traveled with the Redpath Chautauqua for several seasons, limiting his comments to the importance of education for African Americans. Booker T. Washington, the most noted African American of his time, occasionally spoke on the lyceum stage and made several spot appearances on the chautauqua platform. He was a tireless worker for educational opportunities and economic advancement for African Americans, but his approach was conciliatory. He believed in cooperating with the white power structure in achieving his goals, as he had done in establishing Tuskegee Institute with financing from the white community.

Patriotic themes and calls for government reform also played well with chautauqua audiences. Both Warren Harding, while still a senator, and Senator Walter S. Kenyon of Iowa delivered patriotic lectures. The topics selected by other speakers demonstrated the consuming interest in Americanism during and after World War I.

Former governor of Kansas E. W. Hoch toured with chautauqua in 1920 giving a speech called "This Country of Ours." In 1921, Governor Charles H. Brough of Arkansas lectured on "America's world leadership." Following the trend, other speakers covered such subjects as "back to fundamental Americanism" and "keeping America American."

Although programmers avoided speakers espousing radical views, the chautauqua platform was an ideal forum for debates on controversial issues. In 1925 the New York–New England circuit sponsored a debate on League of Nations membership. The topic read: "Resolved, that this House approves of the U.S. continuing to remain outside of the League of Nations." Following the lectures of prominent speakers, an open forum was often scheduled so that members of the audience could ask questions and express their views in an informal setting. With the advent of radio and its rising popularity, chautauqua programs were occasionally broadcast.

Despite the focus on America, chautauqua audiences turned out to hear speeches such as "Awakened China," "The Truth about Mex-

Chautauqua adapts to the new medium of radio. *Chautauqua Collection, Pelletier Library, Allegheny College, Meadville, Pennsylvania.*

ico," "Facts and Fiction in Foreign Affairs," "What about India and World Events?" "Misunderstood Mexico," "The New India," "The Truth about Russia," and "Italy's Place among the Nations."

Residents of chautauqua communities were searching for inspiration and enlightenment, but they also were looking for stories that took them outside the limited orbit of their experience. Sensing this interest, chautauqua management made sure that they booked an occasional travel and adventure program for each summer season. Captain S. K. Gunderson described his twenty-five-hundred-mile exploration across Siberia to awestruck audiences. E. Lorne Knight told of the five months he spent as a member of the Stefansson Arctic Expedition. Mildred Clemens presented an illustrated travelogue, "Rambling through Paradise," which described her trip through the Hawaiian Islands.

In 1930 Carveth Wells, a noted adventurer and author, kept audiences spellbound with his lecture "In Coldest Africa." In it he described the adventures he encountered in 1928 as he explored the

Carveth Wells with fellow explorers Martin and Osa Johnson. *Milwaukee Public Museum Photograph Collection.*

Ruwenzori Range in what was then Central Equatorial Africa. Sometimes referred to as the Mountains of the Moon, the Ruwenzori Range has a year-round cover of snow even though it straddles the equator. Wells had previously established his reputation for adventure after spending six years in the Malay jungle. The popularity of his books and his platform style as a humorous raconteur made him a hit with audiences across the country.

Lady Mary Heath of Ireland, one of aviation's most notable pioneers, toured with Redpath's New York–New England circuit in 1929. During the season Lady Heath flew her own airplane from town

Lady Mary Heath, aviation pioneer and record-holding athlete. *Chautauqua Collection, Pelletier Library, Allegheny College, Meadville, Pennsylvania.*

to town to deliver her lecture "The Conquest of the Air." Her credentials were impressive: She was the first woman to fly from London to Australia. She was holder of the transcontinental speed record for women and holder of the altitude record (24,700 feet) for both men and women. Her most famous flight was in 1928, from Cape Town, South Africa, to Croyden Airport, England, a distance of eleven thousand miles. She had also been the winner of a fifty-mile race for women at the National Air Races in Cleveland.

Lady Heath fascinated chautauqua audiences with tales of her daring exploits. In both Britain and the United States, she became an advocate for travel by air, which she claimed was "the safest means of travel." Ironically, her enthusiasm for aviation proved to be her undoing. In August 1929 she was excused from her lecture schedule for four days to participate in the National Air Races in Cleveland. While practicing maneuvers in preparation for the races, her plane lost power and crashed through a factory roof. A newspaper gave this account of the accident:

> The British woman pilot two days ago came from last to second place in a race in a plane similar to that in which she crashed and her skill in rounding the pylons with vertical banks at that time drew expressions of admiration from other pilots. It was in one of these vertical maneuvers that she crashed, according to witnesses.
>
> She had been stunting the little plane, testing its paces for several minutes, and was coming in for a landing, slipping her plane sideways in a steep descent. Her course lay across the corner of a factory building and almost in line was a tall smokestack. Apparently Lady Heath saw the stack when she was close to it, and in seeking to avert it, miscalculated. Her plane struck the roof with terrific impact and burst through the heavy timbers to the floor below.

Lady Heath's accident was a blow to Redpath's New York–New England circuit because of her popularity as a star attraction. After brain surgery and a long recuperation she was permanently sidelined. As general superintendent, Richie Schultz scrambled to get a replacement for her remaining engagements. Through Crawford Peffer's Redpath Bureau he was successful in lining up Captain Dennis Rooke, another aviator who made aviation history when he flew a tiny, single-engine Moth plane, unaccompanied, on a seven-thousand-mile flight from London to India.

Chautauqua was going to miss the colorful Lady Heath. On a trip to lecture in Cooperstown, New York, she overshot the local airport and landed several miles away at the county poorhouse, to the delight of the elderly inhabitants who had never before seen an airplane land. One of her most remarkable feats was to land a plane while she was unconscious. While flying in South Africa, she fainted while flying alone. She felt faint and had the presence of mind to cut her engine and head the plane for an open space in what she thought was an even glide. She landed safely, but unconscious, and woke up in a hut where natives had revived her.

In addition to being an adventurous flyer, Lady Heath was also a world-renowned athlete who represented Great Britain in track and field events at the Olympic Games. While lecturing on the chautauqua circuit, she still held the world's records for women's high jump and javelin throwing.

Lady Heath and other chautauqua speakers stirred the imagination of the rural populace. Townspeople were transported to the far reaches of the globe as they listened to the stories of Carveth Wells, Drew Pearson, Ruth Bryan Owen, and others. They were mesmerized by the rhetoric of William Jennings Bryan, Russell Conwell, Robert La Follette, and other orators who exposed them to a wide range of new ideas and issues. Chautauqua audiences were swayed by the power and eloquence of their words, just as the Greeks and Romans were swayed by the oratory of Demosthenes, Cato the Elder, and Marc Antony.

Oratory was popular in the tent chautauqua era. Chautauqua listeners savored the words and phrases so carefully crafted by the orators, and that is why they welcomed the opportunity to hear the same speech given year after year by the best of the orators. Chautauqua's speechmakers delivered messages that carried their audiences far beyond their daily routines, and the audiences, left with indelible memories after hearing the chautauqua speakers, enriched the communities in which they lived with their new-found knowledge and perspective.

7

Chautauqua Talent—the Entertainers

Gradually entertainment for the sake of entertainment crept onto the chautauqua stage. Musical groups began to appear in the chautauqua tents, and eventually stage plays were accepted. In the early years small-town audiences had associated the theater and its performers with immorality. Taking the high moral road, chautauqua management had carefully excluded theatrical productions from its program scheduling, but it selectively booked dramatic readings and operatic recitals, which grew in popularity.

British-born actress Eva Le Gallienne, well known to lyceum audiences, was among the dramatic readers who graced the chautauqua platform. In 1920 at the age of twenty-one, Le Gallienne was an immediate hit as the star of Ferenc Molnár's *Liliom* when it played on Broadway. She continued to perform in the dramas of Henrik Ibsen, Anton Chekhov, and other playwrights as her reputation grew. As a multilingual young woman with roots in both England and France, she became acquainted with many of the great literary figures of her day. Among them was Ibsen, for whom she translated seven plays from his native Norwegian. It was natural for her to be drawn to the chautauqua movement as one of its star attractions.

Katharine Ridgeway, another compelling presence on the chautauqua stage, was renowned for her readings of Shakespeare. She married another chautauqua performer, Percy Hunt, who sang with a vocal group, but she eclipsed him in the drawing power of her name as a dramatic reader. Percy Hunt told the story of traveling with

Eva Le Gallienne. *Chautauqua Collection, Pelletier Library, Allegheny College, Meadville, Pennsylvania.*

Katharine Ridgeway Hunt. *Redpath Chautauqua Collection, Special Collections Department, University of Iowa Libraries, Iowa City, Iowa.*

Katharine Ridgeway on a chautauqua circuit in the Midwest. The cowboys would come to the town on horseback, tie up the horses, remove the saddles, and place them on the ground just outside the tent where the flaps of the tent had been raised to allow for air. They would then lounge on the saddles and enjoy a smoke as the performance began. As Percy Hunt told the story, the cowboys paid little attention to the songs rendered by his musical group, but when Katharine Ridgeway came on stage and began her readings, they were riveted and one by one moved to the inside of the tent.

With the demise of circuit chautauqua, Katharine Ridgeway withdrew from her professional career as an elocutionist and moved with her husband to a farm in Coopers Mills, Maine. There she established the Katharine Ridgeway Camp for Girls, a successful venture, which endured for many years. She also raised some of the tastiest blueberries grown in the state of Maine. Meanwhile, she maintained her contacts in the entertainment industry, making occasional trips to Boston for guest appearances and meetings of volunteer boards on which she served.

Sensing that the timing was right, Crawford Peffer, innovative as always, took the risk of booking the Ben Greet Players, renowned for their Shakespeare productions. He calculated correctly that eastern audiences, influenced by their proximity to New York, would be more receptive to the plays, particularly those of Shakespeare, than audiences in other parts of the country. Meanwhile Katharine Ridgeway had done her part in preparing audiences for the beauty of Shakespeare's poetry. Author Betty Fielding comments that elocutionists like Katharine Ridgeway, performing on the Chautauqua stage, introduced her to Shakespeare when she was a very small child in Ligonier, Indiana.

To assure the success of his venture, Peffer hired William Keighley, one of Broadway's top directors. It was the summer of 1913 when Peffer and Keighley introduced the Ben Greet Players in Shakespeare's *Comedy of Errors*, their first chautauqua production. It wasn't long before the comedies and tragedies of Shakespeare were being staged by chautauqua circuits from coast to coast. Following the success with Shakespeare plays, such popular productions as *Abraham Lincoln*, *Journey's End*, *The Goose Hangs High*, *It Pays to Advertise*, and *The Melting Pot* were also introduced to chautauqua audiences. As its title suggests, *The Melting Pot* is a drama that focuses on the vast number

Ben Greet. *Redpath Chautauqua Collection, Special Collections Department, University of Iowa Libraries, Iowa City, Iowa.*

William Keighley. *Schultz Family Chautauqua Collection.*

of immigrants of all nationalities who are fused into a population with a distinctly American identity. These plays and others became one of the most popular features of chautauqua programs.

When the Redpath-Vawter circuit introduced *It Pays to Advertise* to Canton, Missouri, audiences in 1918, it was the first time that the people of Canton had seen a modern drama on the chautauqua stage. Until then Chautauqua Week had exposed them only to short dramatic sketches, one-act plays, and Shakespearian plays. To make sure that the audiences would find the play acceptable, chautauqua management went out of its way to make the point that *It Pays to Advertise* was "absolutely clean and wholesome."

William Keighley, interviewed by the *New York Times* in the spring of 1921, had this to say about the plays scheduled for performance on Chautauqua circuits:

> The season looks very promising. We have under engagement more than 150 actors in companies averaging from seven to ten members. This is the eighth year of the Redpath Bureau in the production of plays

William Keighley (center with cap) and cast of *The Melting Pot. Schultz Family Chautauqua Collection.*

[for Chautauqua]. We began with the Ben Greet Players in Shake-spearian repertoire and now we have enough companies to supply circuits operating from Maine to Florida and as far west and southwest as California and New Mexico. In fact these circuits embrace every State in the Union and there are several other chautauqua bureaus in this same line of work. The towns we play have all the way from 1000 to 75,000 inhabitants, and I have known a town of 900 souls to give us an audience of 1500, the people coming from miles around, as they did last year to Hedrick, Iowa.

Principally it is the church element that supports the chautauqua plays, so you will readily understand our selections must be made with very great care. Many of the towns on the chautauqua circuits have no other form of amusements besides motion pictures. The theater managers, being satisfied with all the gross receipts, are unwilling to experiment with road shows. Hence the chautauqua shows supply the need.

Audiences could be critical if a play did not meet their expectations. In the tiny village of Ransomville, New York, playgoers complained about the all-British cast of *The Perfect Alibi*. They wanted American actors they "could understand."

Humorists were in demand on the chautauqua circuits, but none of them could top Opie Read in popularity. Jess Pugh, who frequently appeared on Vawter's Redpath circuit, was a close second. Opie Read came to chautauqua with an established reputation, not only as a humorist, but as a man of letters. He was a well-known novelist, journalist, and editor who entertained on chautauqua by impersonating characters from his books. The favorite with chautauqua audiences was his impersonation of Lum Jucklin, a homespun farmer who lived in the backwoods of North Carolina. Lum was the protagonist of Read's highly successful novel, *The Jucklins*, which sold over one million copies after it was published in 1896. The locales for most of Read's stories were Kentucky, Alabama, North Carolina, Arkansas, and his home state of Tennessee. With his keen sense of humor, Read was able to capture the quaint philosophy of his characters and bring them to life on the chautauqua stage.

In one passage Lum threatened to kill one of his steers that had kicked him. "I'll blow his head off," said Lum.

His wife responded, "O Limuel, a body to hear you talk would think that you don't do anything at all but thirst for blood."

Author and humorist Opie Read. *Redpath Chautauqua Collection, Special Collections Department, University of Iowa Libraries, Iowa City, Iowa.*

"If the Lord puts it in the mind of a steer to kick you, why, it ain't the poor creeter's fault," Lum snorted. "And if the Lord puts it in my mind to kill the steer it ain't my fault, Mother."

The great orators and inspirational speakers appealed to chautauqua audiences who wanted to be educated, but the large concert bands were the biggest draw for those looking for entertainment. The bands of John Philip Sousa, Bohumir Kryl, Salvatore Ciricillo, and Jaroslav Cimera were headliners known from coast to coast.

George C. Goforth's Black and Gold Band was another of the popular musical groups that toured on chautauqua, primarily in Illinois, Iowa, Minnesota, Missouri, Indiana, Ohio, and West Virginia from 1915 to 1933. In 1924 the *Iowa City Press Citizen* reviewed Goforth's Iowa City concert in the August 14 edition of the newspaper:

> The concert program was varied and selections to please the most fastidious were played. "Humoresque," "Prelude" by Rachmaninoff and "Onward Christian Soldiers" provided a variety of quick moving music. The Goforthers had all the necessary instruments for noise-making. Mr. Goforth himself performed on the two big drums, which looked like new electric washing machines, and on the xylophone.

Goforth's son, J. Austin Goforth, often traveled with his father on the summer circuits. He reminisced about his experience:

> Chautauquas were held usually in big tents, sometimes in auditoriums. It was an event looked forward to year after year. Farm families would come in and stay several days at a time. They rode often in grain wagons drawn by horses, with a wealth of farm food stored inside to last them. Farm life in those days was drudgery. The chautauquas gave these isolated lonely people an outlet for their emotions, as well as a lot of fresh things to think about the following winter. They appreciated what we did for them. Their whoops and applause following some number that especially pleased them were so loud and so long, I think they could have been heard miles away! Goforth's Black and Gold concerts were very solid performances, ranging from fine overtures through military marches to the popular hit tunes of the day. Dad always played xylophone solos, including "American Patrol March," *Poet and Peasant Overture* by Von Suppe, and "Hungarian Dance Number Five."

Bohumir Kryl (left) and Opie Read. *Redpath Chautauqua Collection, Special Collections Department, University of Iowa Libraries, Iowa City, Iowa.*

Cast of *The Mikado. Lewis County, Missouri, Historical Society.*

A host of miscellaneous entertainers, including magicians, puppeteers, and dancers, added to the variety of entertainment that became a staple of chautauqua programs. Musicians brought grand and light opera. The light opera productions of Victor Herbert and Gilbert and Sullivan were always well received, starting with a performance of *The Mikado* on Vawter's Midwest circuit for the first time in 1914.

As a child in Coshocton, Ohio, Miriam Mellen was fascinated by the opportunities provided by chautauqua to, as she puts it, "nurture my cultural experience." She was fascinated by a group of Russian folk dancers with their colorful costumes. She remembers tumblers and jugglers and was particularly impressed with an entertainer who played both the Jew's harp and the ocarina. Miriam enjoyed the music, in all of its diversity, including the group singing occasionally led

Women Members of the Fortune Tellers Chorus, 1927. *Schultz Family Chautauqua Collection.*

from the stage by one of the performers. Her friend, Marge Hallock, credits chautauqua for introducing her as a youngster to a wide range of music.

To provide a light touch in an otherwise serious program, it was customary to schedule musical entertainment before the introduction of a featured lecturer. Among the many choral and instrumental groups who served in this capacity was a popular group of sixteen singers, both men and women, known as "The Fortune Tellers Chorus." Another group of talented entertainers was the Ionian Serenaders, who toured for several seasons with the Ellison-White Chautauqua. They were an ensemble of four versatile young women, each of whom played the accordion as a concert instrument and sang a repertoire of familiar songs. One of them also played the cello and another the violin.

The arrival of chautauqua was eagerly anticipated by a few local amateurs who sensed an opportunity to break into show business. In one town there was a little girl who did both serious and humorous

Superintendent Eben Schultz with members of the Fortune Tellers Chorus.
Schultz Family Chautauqua Collection.

readings. Her mother and friends insisted that she was just as talented as the professional readers appearing that week on the chautauqua stage. Through their connections with the Chautauqua Committee, they prevailed on the superintendent to let her audition. The result was disastrous. It hadn't occurred to the mother that the professionals to whom she was comparing her daughter had trained for years before they developed the stage presence and confidence to appear before an audience as accomplished performers.

In Lancaster, Missouri, a male quartet, the pride of that little community of less than a thousand people, offered to sing at the opening of the week's chautauqua program. The local committee assured Superintendent Eben Schultz that this group would "wow" the audience and even suggested that they be given a contract to tour on one of the chautauqua circuits. Even though it was contrary to custom, Eben agreed to let the quartet start the program. Unused to the cavernous tent and such a large audience, the four men became hopelessly lost on the first number and never recovered. They sounded weak, flat, and colorless. Eben was embarrassed and vowed never again to suc-

The Ionian Serenaders, 1916. *Oregon Historical Society (MSS-1530)*.

cumb to the pressure of hometown boosters of local talent. Having learned his lesson, he was better prepared when a local minister with a prominent guarantor confronted him with a request to book him for a summer season to deliver a patriotic lecture. He conveniently arranged his own audition, presenting the lecture at a Sunday morning service in his church and inviting the chautauqua staff to attend. Eben said that the "results were gruesome." The talk was too long, inappropriate for chautauqua, contained few ideas, no humor, and no entertainment value. Eben finessed that one by telling him he would write up a report and send it to Mr. Vawter.

With performers, many of them temperamental and demanding, there were often problems to be resolved, and that job fell to that jack-

A vocal ensemble in patriotic garb. *Chautauqua Collection, Pelletier Library, Allegheny College, Meadville, Pennsylvania.*

of-all-trades, the chautauqua superintendent, known to crew members as "The Supe." It might have been a troupe of Russian singers who often quarreled among themselves about their accommodations, or it could have been a bandleader who insisted that his musicians receive top billing over a noted inspirational speaker. It was usually "The Supe," in another of his roles, who mediated the dispute.

Charles Starrett created embarrassment for Superintendent Eben Schultz when chautauqua played Albion, New York, in 1927. Starrett was a promising and handsome young actor who had recently graduated from Dartmouth. He liked to party and was known as a free spirit. Celebrating in Albion after one of his shows, he arrived back at the hotel, pleasantly inebriated, and drifted into a room assigned to some of the girls in the show. He took off his clothes, drew a bath, and stepped into the bathtub. It was there that the hotel manager found him, singing Dartmouth fraternity songs at the top of his lungs. In the thirties Starrett gravitated to Hollywood, where he was featured in a number of class-B Westerns and starred in *So Red the Rose,* a box office success of the thirties.

A different problem for the "Supe" was created when a fire destroyed the tent on the first day of Chautauqua Week in the town of Newark, New York. The local newspaper gave this account of the incident:

> Fire believed to be the fault of defective wiring swept the huge tent housing the Newark Chautauqua late this afternoon, destroying the canvas, electrical equipment, seats, scenery, and a piano at a loss of $5000. Bursting out along the canvas, the flames converted the tent into a giant torch and completed their work of destruction in fifteen minutes. Firemen arrived to find the place leveled.

Superintendent David Cook quickly arranged for the remaining performances to be held in Newark's Park Presbyterian Church. Junior Chautauqua activities were shifted to the high school gymnasium.

With the outbreak of World War I, the Redpath Chautauquas participated in a program to provide entertainment for servicemen in training camps, including the loan of tents and related equipment. Unlike permanent assembly halls, the big brown tents could be moved from one location to another to accommodate the requirements of the military.

Despite the popularity of chautauqua, there were a few detractors. Santa Fe, New Mexico, hosted the Redpath-Horner Chautauqua from 1916 to 1918, but there was strong resistance when a group of out-of-state women promoted the creation of a permanent chautauqua or "culture colony," as they referred to it, in Santa Fe in 1926. In his article "Chautauquas: Caravans of Culture," Richard Melzer, professor of history at the University of New Mexico in Los Lunas, describes the furor generated by the proposal:

> Led by artists and authors such as Mary Austin, Carlos Vierra, Joseph G. Bakos, John Sloan, and Sinclair Lewis, those who opposed the Chautauqua argued that such a proposal would unduly compromise Santa Fe's peaceful, traditional setting. According to Lewis, "it would be a ghastly mishap to hand the town over to the hordes of seekers for predigested culture—to change it from a dignified and distinguished city into a flimsy fairground."

Mexican dancers pose for a snapshot with Eben Schultz.
Chautauqua Collection, Pelletier Library, Allegheny College, Meadville, Pennsylvania.

Military personnel assembled in a chautauqua tent. *Chautauqua Collection, Pelletier Library, Allegheny College, Meadville, Pennsylvania.*

Dr. Melzer writes that a cultural war ensued. Opponents organized the Old Santa Fe Association to preserve "the unique charm and distinction of the city" against the " 'thundering hordes.' " Despite support from the city's chamber of commerce and other groups, the chautauqua proponents withdrew their plans and moved the project to Las Vegas, New Mexico.

Across the country in Moravia, New York, the Redpath Chautauqua in 1928 ran into opposition led by the manager of the local movie theater, who had rented an old stagecoach, plastered it with his ads, and drove it all over town, especially on the nights when plays were scheduled at the chautauqua tent. Superintendent Eben Schultz gave him a complimentary chautauqua ticket in an appeal for his cooperation, but he was unyielding. The harassment continued but didn't seem to affect chautauqua attendance.

John D. Rockefeller had grown up in Moravia, and in his later years he returned for an annual visit to immerse himself in nostalgia. During Chautauqua Week in 1928, several of the tent crew observed Rockefeller riding along Main Street, throwing dimes to children as he went. It was one of his favorite pastimes.

In the early years of the traveling chautauquas, educational programs took precedence over entertainment. Speakers were the main

Boosters' Club

Believing in Chautauqua, and desiring that Moravia may continue to enjoy its many benefits, I hereby agree to purchase . . . . adult and . . . . . children's season tickets before the opening of the Chautauqua in Moravia in 1928.

_____
Name

R. D. _____
Address

A boosters' club promoted chautauqua in Moravia, New York. *Schultz Family Chautauqua Collection.*

attraction. Serious lectures were preceded by lighter musical inter-ludes to prepare an audience for the main event, and sometimes a mu-sical number would follow a lecture.

As the musical offerings improved in quality and grew in variety, chautauqua management began to feature them more prominently. Light opera, with selections from Gilbert and Sullivan, big concert bands, vocal ensembles such as the Fisk Jubilee Singers, and soloists of the stature of Madame Schumann-Heink, began to appear as fea-tured performers — but top billing continued to go to the inspirational and oratorical speakers.

Drama, with its perceived aura of immorality, was frowned upon in the early days. Elocutionists such as Katharine Ridgeway and Eva Le Gallienne, reading from Shakespeare and Ibsen, conditioned au-diences to appreciate theatrical performances. Nevertheless, the ora-tors remained paramount. With an acute sense of timing, Crawford Peffer contracted for England's famed Ben Greet Players to bring Shakespeare's plays to the chautauqua stage in America. It was only a matter of time before stage plays became a staple of chautauqua pro-gramming. Eventually, chautauqua attenders could expect a blend of both educational features and entertainment; however, even though lectures continued to be the most compelling attraction, some historians claim that an overemphasis on entertainment contributed to the demise of circuit chautauquas.

8

Junior Chautauqua

Children figured prominently in the success of the traveling chautauquas. From the start, chautauqua management encouraged families with children to attend. Townspeople insisted on a full range of children's activities as part of the chautauqua contract. Programs designed specifically for children were organized and supervised by an experienced professional often called the "story lady," "junior girl," or "children's supervisor." The Junior Chautauqua extended through the week and included a mix of education and entertainment that appealed to children. Typically the junior program contained elements of supervised play, citizenship training, nature studies, storytelling, athletic contests, and woodcraft.

To stimulate interest in the children's program, the advance agent often conducted a "ticket hunt" for the children of the community. The lucky finders of season tickets were the envy of their friends, who would badger their parents for money to buy their own tickets.

On the morning of the first day, the story lady met with the boys and girls who were fortunate enough to have tickets. The activities of the week were outlined and a preview of the junior program was presented. Often superimposed on the schedule of daily activities was a project that occupied the children during the week with a grand finale on the final day.

Pageants were a favorite, with the children auditioning, rehearsing, and selecting their costumes during the week and performing before the full chautauqua audience on the final day. Costumes were

Junior Chautauqua participants. *Chautauqua Collection, Pelletier Library, Allegheny College, Meadville, Pennsylvania.*

provided by the chautauqua staff. With so many children involved, the pageant was guaranteed to be a sellout performance. Among the favorite productions were *Mother Goose Party; County Fair; Little Olde Folkes Concert* (with "the songs ye grandmothers used to sing; likewise some other merrie things such as drills and pretty pantomimes"); *America Triumphant* (showing highlights in American history); *The Magic Piper* (a dramatization of the Pied Piper Story); and *World Wide Peace* (a pageant with music). In the country's sesquicentennial year, 1926, the children performed in *The Bell*. It was a pageant "depicting scenes from the stirring times of 150 years ago which centered about the ringing of the Liberty Bell at the signing of the Declaration of Independence."

Sometimes the children's project was a parade, with bands, floats, clowns, and dancers, for which preparations were made throughout the week. The most popular project, particularly with parents, was "Junior Town," a form of citizenship training. On the first day of Chautauqua Week, the children met with the story lady and orga-

Children in costume for a Junior Chautauqua pageant. *Chautauqua Collection, Pelletier Library, Allegheny College, Meadville, Pennsylvania.*

Dressed for a Junior Chautauqua parade in Woodsville, New Hampshire. *Schultz Family Chautauqua Collection.*

nized a municipal government. Elections were held for mayor, chief of police, town clerk, and other officials. Marge Hallock of Pleasant Hill, California, remembers her participation in Junior Town when chautauqua visited her hometown of Union City, Pennsylvania. When the elections were held, Marge became the Junior Town mayor, a distinctive achievement for an eighth grade student. Once the officers had been installed, town meetings were held every morning in the tent. Laws were enacted that dealt initially with the chautauqua environment but later with community issues. Richie Schultz told of one town's actual legislation to eliminate an unsightly city dump, which had resulted from a "Junior Town" initiative. In another town a permanent playground was established when the children of "Junior Town" called attention to the lack of playground facilities in the community.

The story lady made sure that parliamentary procedures were observed and emphasized the importance of good sportsmanship in discussion and debate. The Junior Town song, of dubious poetic merit but carrying an important message, was learned early in the week and sung at each town meeting session:

> I am proud of my town,
> Is my town proud of me?
> What she needs are citizens
> Trained in loyalty.
> When we work, when we play
> With our fellow men,
> Good citizens we will be.
> Then I'll be proud,
> Be proud of my home town,
> And I'll make her proud of me.

Another project used as an alternative to "Junior Town" was known as Seton Indian work. It involved woodcrafting programs based on the ideas of Ernst Thompson Seton, a naturalist, author, and artist, and a cofounder of the Boy Scouts of America. Based on Native American culture and ideals, the project was presented in a chautauqua brochure as "a combination of instruction and wholesome fun":

> Two tribes of Indians will be organized. Indian names and dress will be adopted and the Indians of J. Fenimore Cooper of Leather-Stocking

Children prepared to take part in Seton Indian work. *State Historical Society of Missouri, Columbia.*

fame will be taken as the type. Honor, fairness, courage, and clean living will be emphasized. Interesting legends of the Hiawatha character will be told. There will be Indian songs and games, bow and arrow practice, out of door jaunts, natural history observations, health talks, war whoops and a merry lot more to fill young hearts to the brim and put the rosy blush of health in the cheeks.

The story lady had received special training to make the program uniform in each town. Only children between the ages of six and fourteen who held season tickets to chautauqua were eligible to participate. On the Ellison-White circuit, the story lady donned appropriate attire to become an "Indian princess" while she conducted the Seton Indian project. In towns where the project was included in the chautauqua program, the tent crews referred to the story lady as "the Squaw."

Junior Chautauqua played a significant role in the development of the Boy Scouts of America and Camp Fire USA. In 1911, at a time when these youth organizations were in their infancy, a Redpath-Vawter Chautauqua program included this item:

Poster promoting Junior Chautauqua. *Chautauqua Collection, Pelletier Library, Allegheny College, Meadville, Pennsylvania.*

The Boy Scout idea is sweeping over the country like wildfire. It is only a year old and already 400,000 boys are enlisted in this wonderful peace movement. Who can guess what another year's growth will add?

Not to be outdone, the girls of America are springing a movement of similar character, known as Camp-Fire Girls. One of the objects is to encourage outdoor exercise and promote health. Both movements contemplate trips to the fields and woods and good times galore. Our Scout Director has adapted the work of the two movements so they will go nicely together, and is planning to give the newly organized Boy Scouts and Camp-Fire Girls of this community the time of their lives. Any boy or girl with a child's season ticket may become a member.

A junior program announced in 1910 as "the greatest child feature ever attempted by a chautauqua management" was King Arthur's Court. In this program the mornings were given over to learning the Arthurian legends and enacting them on the chautauqua stage. On the first day, a King Arthur was elected by vote of the children and the parts of the various knights were assigned. Appropriate costumes, banners, shields, swords, coats of armor, lances, and helmets were made available to the children to add authenticity to the stage presentations. There were also tournaments, games, and romantic stories of the days of chivalry. The advance team worked with the local chautauqua committee to brief the children of the community on the Arthurian legends before chautauqua came to town. A search for the Holy Grail "in imitation of Arthur's men" was the climax of the week's activity.

In 1916 the Redpath-Horner circuit introduced a children's Chautauqua Circus, complete with wild animals, acrobats, clowns, and, of course, a parade. The Ellison-White Chautauqua also featured a circus for children.

Most of the supervised play, participation in Junior Town, and preparation for parades and theatrical productions took place in the afternoons. The morning hours featured the professional entertainers: magicians, jugglers, impersonators, circus clowns, performing dogs, and bird trainers. Marionettes and Punch-and-Judy shows were also popular with the children. Among the many performers appearing on the Junior Chautauqua program was a young ventriloquist named Edgar Bergen. Bergen made his first appearance in 1923 on Redpath's southern circuit. He was still a nineteen-year-old student at Northwestern University at the time.

Oh Kiddies, Kiddies, Just Look Here!

We have got it now. Say, do you know that we have got it all fixed up for you youngsters to put on a circus performance night under the big Chautauqua tent?

Well, we have. And it isn't going to be any make believe circus either. It will be a real one, with plenty of the funniest wild animals you ever saw.

You kiddies are going to have the fun of making most of the wild animals, and of training them too. The play supervisor will teach you how. There will be lions, giraffes, ostriches, gooks, monkeys and all sorts, big and little.

The most elaborate, elastic, enthralling, engaging, engrossing, entertaining, enterprising, and enthusing institution ever inaugurated. Such a lot of fun for the boys and girls never was seen before anywhere.

PUT ON A CIRCUS ASSISTED BY RENO

It will take near a week of joyful work and play to get the menagerie and circus ready. Then you will put it on under the big tent.

Ringmaster, clowns, acrobats, performing animals, specialty artists, all fixed up circus fashion, will do their stunts. Oh, it will be piles and piles of fun.

And Reno, the great magician, will happen along and help out on the show. He is the cleverest trickster you ever heard tell of. He will put on the finishing touches.

It's a scream. It's a dream. It's a whirlwind team. Every boy and girl for miles around will want to help build and put on this circus, and make it a great big success.

Excerpt from a Junior Chautauqua program. *Chautauqua Collection, Pelletier Library, Allegheny College, Meadville, Pennsylvania.*

Edgar Bergen with Charlie McCarthy and Charlie's sister, Laura. *Redpath Chautauqua Collection, Special Collections Department, University of Iowa Libraries, Iowa City, Iowa.*

Bergen was a big hit with his dummies Charlie McCarthy and Charlie's sister, Laura, but Charlie was so popular that Laura was soon dropped from the act. Billed as an attraction for children, Bergen was soon drawing a sizable following, not only from the children, but also from their parents. As the superintendent on the southern circuit, it was Richie Schultz's job to introduce Bergen. They remained good friends long after Bergen had moved on to radio and the movies.

Magicians were a staple on Junior Chautauqua shows. Children responded to their amazing tricks with rapt attention and fascination. On the winter circuit in which Edgar Bergen made his debut, I traveled with my parents as we moved from town to town while my father functioned as the circuit manager. At age three, I often served as a foil for the magician who performed on the children's program. Perched in a front-row seat, I would respond to the magician's call for volunteers to "assist" him and run up to the stage. Miraculously, the magician would pull yards of colored bunting from my shirt. It was a show business debut that had no lasting consequences.

The children's programs were well attended because chautauqua was perceived as a family affair. It could have been that some chil-

The author (age three) waiting for a train to the next chautauqua town. *Schultz Family Chautauqua Collection.*

dren were dragged kicking and screaming to the big brown tents, but once there, they were richly rewarded with nonstop entertainment. To attract other children, as well as their parents, Crawford Peffer sometimes enlisted the help of his little daughter to sell season tickets.

Floy Welch, an adventurous young woman from Eldora, Iowa, joined Keith Vawter's Redpath Chautauqua as a story lady for the summer season of 1918. During the winter months Floy was an art teacher at a local college. Floy crossed paths with Eben Schultz when the two of them were working on chautauqua in Ellendale, North Dakota. Eben had been sent as the advance man for the Ellendale Chautauqua and Floy was the story lady, in charge of the children's program. Eben first spotted Floy in a hotel dining room and was captivated. His first impression was confirmed when he watched Floy lead the parade of her Junior Chautauqua charges down the main street of town. He arranged for an introduction and from that moment took every opportunity to meet with her.

In Alexandria, Minnesota, later in the summer, Eben had the good fortune (or was it prearranged?) to be the chautauqua superintendent with Floy as his cashier. (The story lady often doubled as the cashier.) During the week in Alexandria, he almost ruined his chances with Floy when he missed their dinner date at the local hotel. The Alexandria school superintendent had taken him for a sightseeing drive and failed to get him back in time for dinner. Eben finally showed up while a miffed Floy was having dessert. It may have been a setback for the romance, but not for long. During the 1919 season, while Eben was managing the chautauqua program in Elbow Lake, Minnesota, with Floy again as the cashier, she accepted his fraternity pin, and the engagement was on. They were married in September 1920 at the end of the chautauqua season. After three years of travel on Vawter's Redpath circuit, Floy retired to establish a household in Eben's hometown of Canton, Missouri.

Most of the local children were well behaved, particularly those who attended Junior Chautauqua, but there were always a few young ruffians who hung around the chautauqua grounds with the intent of creating a disturbance. They were a minority, but one of Eben Schultz's property men found a way to deal with them. He enlisted them as part of his crew to go after others who might cause trouble. Eben cited the case of Dolgeville, New York, where there had been

Story lady Floy Welch. *Schultz Family Chautauqua Collection.*

Gathering of story ladies. *Redpath Chautauqua Collection, Special Collections Department, University of Iowa Libraries, Iowa City, Iowa.*

Lining up for a Junior Chautauqua parade. *Chautauqua Collection, Pelletier Library, Allegheny College, Meadville, Pennsylvania.*

problems from a fringe element each time chautauqua came to town. The local "enforcer" recruited by the crew promised to control the situation and he did. He was a cocky youngster and addressed Eben with "Hi, Chief."

Junior Chautauqua was introduced to the movement by Paul Pearson, founder of the Swarthmore Chautauqua. It was soon a standard feature of chautauqua programs and represented a significant contribution to the financial success and popularity of tent chautauquas. Attendance became a family affair, with incentives for both parents and children to participate.

Small communities were family oriented and valued the opportunity to expose their children to cultural programs that were both educational and entertaining: Junior Town taught them citizenship; the big concert bands and musical ensembles taught them to appreciate good music; and the pageants in which they participated introduced them to theatrical performance. Parents valued the supervised play that chautauqua provided.

Junior Chautauqua was an integral part of Chautauqua Week, and it was also a criterion used by the local committee in determining whether to renew the contract for the following year. Meanwhile, chautauqua management was motivated to provide the most qualified junior supervisors and most talented performers, to measure up to community expectations.

Children engage in Seton Indian work. *Redpath Chautauqua Collection, Special Collections Department, University of Iowa Libraries, Iowa City, Iowa.*

9

The Demise of Circuit Chautauquas

Chautauqua gave Richie and Eben the opportunity to rub shoulders with Bryan, La Follette, Harding, and the many other dignitaries who performed on the chautauqua stage. Some of them, like poet Lew Sarett and dramaturge William Kieghley, became lifelong friends. Chautauqua was an education not only for the small-town audiences it served but also for the staff and crew members. As English professors, both Richie and Eben were able to enrich their college courses with the firsthand exposure they had with some of the world's most interesting personalities. It is remarkable that the men and women of prominence who toured with chautauqua were willing to put up with life on the road, traveling from town to town on one-night stands, enduring the discomforts of substandard hotels, subsisting on mediocre meals, losing sleep, and relying on trains that rarely ran on time. It was not the life to which they were accustomed, but there was a fascination with chautauqua they could not resist.

Although Peffer's well-managed New York–New England circuit continued to prosper through the 1920s, the seeds of circuit chautauqua's demise had already been sown across the country. There was a gradual erosion of chautauqua audiences despite the efforts of chautauqua's impresarios to improve and alter the content and quality of their product. The Ellison-White circuit, in an effort to resuscitate chautauqua in the west, appealed to the unique sense of community that chautauqua created among its audiences. It also upgraded and diversified its presentations. When the Ellison-White Chautauqua play-

Melting Pot cast copes with the hardships of the nomad life. *Schultz Family Chautauqua Collection.*

ed Dallas, Oregon, in 1928, the program had this to say regarding the influence of competitive forces:

> Chautauqua is keeping pace with the metamorphosis that has been changing the world into a new and better one in recent years. Hard roads, luxurious cars, radio, superb talking machines, air mail and travel, homes that rival the palaces of old time kings, only serve to emphasize the fact that after all, it is friendship and human understanding and religion and family love, personal contact with great thinkers and teachers and artists that give life its beauty and happiness.
>
> Nothing has been devised to bring the whole community together as happily, as cheaply, and for as worthwhile a purpose, as chautauqua. It is community playtime—the finest fun of the year. Hundreds of cities have tried doing without chautauqua in recent years and then have come back to the circuits to save their community souls.

Ellison-White's optimism and salvage efforts could not alter the inexorable forces that were sealing the fate of the traveling chautauquas. The crash of 1929 was a crowning blow they were not able to survive. The Swarthmore Chautauqua, plagued with the problems of declining audiences and financial losses, declared bankruptcy in 1930.

As horse and buggy gave way to the automobile, chautauqua attendance began to wane. *Schultz Family Chautauqua Collection.*

Many reasons have been advanced for the dwindling support of a movement that had been wildly popular for so many years. The *New York Times* speculated that "every invention from the automobile to electronic communications and mass higher education seems to have helped kill all the parts of the circuit but its heart," referring to the mother institution in Chautauqua, New York. Indeed, with its stable roots and long history dating back to 1874, the Chautauqua Institution, located in Chautauqua, New York, continues to thrive to this day.

The automobile and better roads made it possible to journey from the small towns to the big cities for similar entertainment and educational opportunities. Radio was spreading rapidly and it was no longer necessary to wait for Chautauqua Week for fresh programs and new ideas. The radio brought the messages of statesmen and spiritual leaders right into the home. Edgar Bergen began to broadcast his conversations with his puppet Charlie McCarthy. Radio drama and the movies began to compete with chautauqua's stage plays, reaching an ever-widening audience. Meanwhile public tastes were changing.

Winter scene on the campus of the Chautauqua Institution. *Chautauqua Institution Archives, Chautauqua, New York.*

The oratorical style of a William Jennings Bryan began to seem dated. Crawford Peffer, in a letter to Eben Schultz, commented that Senator La Follette had been a hit in the big cities during the winter lyceum season, but the small towns on the summer chautauqua circuit showed little interest in booking him. As Peffer said, "They would rather see their money spent on the entertainments than on the lecturers, so we are going ahead on that basis."

As the interests of community leaders began to expand beyond the boundaries of the towns in which they lived, it became more difficult for chautauqua managers to rally the local support they needed to make their annual visits a financial success. Reacting to declining gate receipts, Keith Vawter, in a letter to his managers, wrote "I still insist that the radio did not materially affect lyceum and chautauquas, but rather the advent of Country Clubs and Dancing Mothers." A more plausible reason, however, was the proliferation of chautauqua circuits, which stepped up the competition for talent and consequently caused an overall decline in quality. Another contributing factor, and a significant one, was the financial crash of 1929, which plunged the country into the Great Depression. Many communities were so finan-

The Redpath Chautauqua visits Adams, New York. *Schultz Family Chautauqua Collection (Lee McClean photo).*

cially strapped that they could not provide the guarantees required by chautauqua circuits.

Peffer's New York–New England circuit managed to buck the trend through the 1920s, and Peffer was convinced that it could survive the lean years of the thirties. In a letter to Eben Schultz in February 1932, he stated "I am sure if we can keep chautauqua going in New York and New England until the depression is over that this circuit will go merrily on its way for many years to come." To garner support he wrote a letter to the committee chairmen in each chautauqua town, asking for suggestions to bolster the program and assure its future. On March 2, 1932, Peffer responded to a reply he had received from the chairman of the Camden, New York, committee, and told him:

> I am rather disappointed to find that the great majority suggest that for the coming summer it would be better to have the program made up of plays and light entertainments. . . .
> Most of those who prefer to have a speaker prominent in public life oppose the suggestion of Senator La Follette. Three have said they would not go to hear him were he on the program. A leading lawyer

in Plattsburgh, New York, writes as follows: "I am inclined to believe that it would be well to have three good plays. Personally, I am not very fond of Senator La Follette's political ideas, and if he is brought in as a lecturer in a certain sense it is an endorsement of him."

So it seems that many people of conservative beliefs are opposed to hearing discussed the Progressive side of public questions. . . . You would be surprised to know how few of the men prominent in the House and Senate can give a good lecture. A lecture must be much more substantial than a speech.

But Peffer wasn't quite so sanguine when he wrote to Eben in June 1933:

It has now been definitely decided that chautauqua on our New York and New England Circuit will be omitted for the coming summer.

While everyone has been more hopeful since March 4, conditions have not yet actually improved, and what finally influenced us to carry the chautauqua contracts over instead of going ahead with the program which we had arranged for this summer was the fact that just about three weeks ago a large number of banks closed in New England; twelve in Maine, two in Gardiner and two in Augusta. I think it would have been almost impossible to have done anything with chautauqua in New England this summer.

So far, all but nine towns have taken the necessary steps to carry their contracts over. Of the remaining nine, only three have refused, so all told, I do not think we will lose more than five or six towns by switching the contracts over to 1934.

In Farmington, Maine, where for many years long lines used to form to buy season tickets, it became a struggle to muster community support for chautauqua. Dick Mallett, in his *History of Farmington*, described the situation: "Near the end of the twenties it became increasingly difficult to sell tickets, and only the zeal of a few saved it until it expired in 1932. My father was enthusiastic about chautauqua to the very end. If his son went to a ball game, instead of an educational presentation under the tent, he treated the incident the same way he would have if his son had skipped school." There was increasing indifference on the part of local citizens; even the strong support of Mr. Mallett and others could not overcome it in their efforts to keep chautauqua alive.

The depression deepened and a 1934 season never materialized. The New York–New England circuit of the Redpath Chautauquas played its last season in 1932. The final performance took place in Portsmouth, New Hampshire, on September 1. The six-day program had included a popular science lecture by scientist Dr. Luther S. H. Gable entitled "The Astonishing Story of Radium." Robert M. Zimmerman had given a speech called "On the Bottom of the Sea," and Roy L. Smith had delivered an inspirational message, "At the Foot of the Rainbow." Also on the program was John Bockewitz with a presentation called "High Lights and Shadows," which included pictures and comedy sketches. Capping off the week's program on the final night was a highly popular Broadway hit, *The Show Off*, directed by William Keighley.

Anna Lauers Matthews, Crawford Peffer's assistant at Redpath headquarters, described the mood of chautauqua patrons after the curtain fell on the last performance: "The grass was wet with dew, and they shivered on that night of September 1932 at Portsmouth, New Hampshire. They stood in prayer-like silence as they watched the big tent slowly, quietly lowered to the ground. No one spoke while the sections were unlaced, folded, and put in the dray wagon to be taken to the waiting baggage car. Each walked slowly away to his home." It was a solemn occasion for those to whom Chautauqua Week had become an annual ritual.

A last attempt was made by C. Benjamin Franklin of Associated Chautauquas to resuscitate the dying cultural phenomenon. In 1933 he raised a tent in Keota, Iowa, for the performance of three plays. It was a futile effort that brought an end to a brilliant chapter of America's cultural history. Historian Richard Melzer, writing on the circuit chautauqua movement, made a discerning observation:

> Having admirably filled a cultural void for many years, chautauqua became a cultural anachronism, drowned in a tidal wave of cultural change whose great impact eventually reached far-off New Mexico. Gone, but much appreciated for their contributions to an earlier age, chautauqua's dedicated performers and local sponsors richly deserve a final chautauqua salute.

The circuit chautauquas may have folded, but in New York State the Chautauqua Institution continues to flourish, attracting talent and audiences from all over the country for its lengthy summer season. Elsewhere, copying the success of the "mother" institution, independent chautauquas, using permanent facilities and campgrounds, con-

Anna Lauers Matthews. *Schultz Family Chautauqua Collection.*

tinue to offer varied cultural and religious programs on a more modest scale. At one time there were over 350 independents, many with limited resources, but offering a diverse mix of program content. Without the economies of scale that the circuit chautauquas were able to achieve with multiple venues in the form of tents, the independents were at a disadvantage in competing for top-quality talent. Despite their ups and downs, many of them were able to survive, retaining their individuality and developing strong support from regional audiences.

Oregon was a fertile field for the chautauqua movement. The independent Willamette Valley Chautauqua was established in 1900 in Oregon City, where a permanent facility was built in Gladstone Park. It featured a program of lecturers, elocutionists, readers, humorists, singers, and cartoonists during the summer months. Another independent, the Southern Oregon Chautauqua Assembly, was established in Ashland, Oregon, a forerunner of the Ashland Shakespeare Festival,

Pavillion at the Willamette Valley Chautauqua in Gladstone Park, Oregon City, Oregon. *Oregon Historical Society (OrHi 89095 #444).*

which has now become a year-round attraction. Competition for talent and patrons eventually undermined support for the Oregon independents. In 1981 a revival was attempted with moderate success. Sponsored by the Oregon Committee for the Humanities, it involved a mix of cultural events that toured throughout the state to "relive the chautauqua days of the early 1900s when lecturers and performers traveled the back roads of America." It closed after a disappointing season in 1985.

In 1984 the Michigan Council for the Humanities celebrated its tenth anniversary with a symposium called "American Culture and the Chautauqua Era, 1874–1932." The council had invited leading scholars to address the impact of chautauqua on American life. Their comments were later reported in a special issue of the *Henry Ford Museum and Greenfield Village Herald*. A significant part of the celebration was the re-creation of a tent chautauqua of the year 1912. A large tent was raised in Greenfield Village and a succession of speakers impersonated prominent historical figures who were featured on the chautauqua platform during the early part of the century. The chautauqua was staged for six days, from May 8 to 13. In the interests of authenticity, the chautauqua offered the same diversity found in the chautauqua programs of 1912.

The education provided by stirring speakers was balanced with entertainment by musicians, dramatic readers, and magicians. The student groups and other attenders experienced the thrill of listening to William Jennings Bryan, Jane Addams, Theodore Roosevelt, Clarence Darrow, and others, all of whom were portrayed by actors. They heard an impersonator deliver the Reverend Russell Conwell's famous "Acres of Diamonds" speech, and another, assuming the role of humorist Opie Read, kept the audience in stitches with his backwoods philosophy. Reflecting on the success of the Greenfield Village chautauqua, Harold K. Skramstad Jr., president of the Edison Institute, wrote that "the most important impact of our Chautauqua was its reaffirmation, in the true Chautauqua spirit, of the value of informed, public education in the humanities as a central feature of a democratic society."

Today there are well over thirty independent chautauquas located in almost as many states. Their programs vary in length from weekends to one week or longer. Only a few have the summerlong scope of the Chautauqua Institution in New York State. The Ocean Park

Actor portraying General Ulysses S. Grant in a 1926 chautauqua production of *Abraham Lincoln. Schultz Family Chautauqua Collection.*

Association in Ocean Park, Maine, runs daily programs from the end of May to early September. Founded in 1881 under the auspices of the Free Will Baptists, it was also known as the Eastern New England Chautauqua, for its program was modeled after the cultural format of the Chautauqua Institution. Its charter stated that it was established as "a place of summer resort for holding religious, educational and other meetings."

Another existing chautauqua organization is the Colorado Chautauqua, which had its origins in 1898 and operates a summer program on its own premises in Boulder. Started as an educational retreat for teachers from Texas, it retains its educational orientation but also includes theatrical and musical events in its programming. The Bay View Association in Petosky, Michigan, has an active chautauqua program that includes musicals, plays, opera, vesper concerts, and youth activities under a director of religious activities. It began at the turn of the century with programs concentrating on travelogues, art, poetry, and literature. The recently revived Chautauqua Center in De Funiak Springs, Florida, sponsors weekend assemblies that include craft demonstrations and workshops, theological lectures, and dramatizations. Many of the independent chautauqua sites are now preserved in the National Historic Register of Historic Places.

Eschewing any formal relationships with each other for many years, a majority of the independents are now in communication through the Network of Chautauquas, which was organized in 1983. The network, holding occasional meetings and producing a biennial newsletter, facilitates a synergistic exchange of ideas and information from which all of the members benefit. Today's independent chautauqua movement is undergoing a revival, creating a strong cultural presence from coast to coast. With better transportation and the "retreat" environment offered by most of the independents, their reach and appeal makes them a viable alternative to the cultural resources of large urban centers.

As a contemporary expression of Keith Vawter's traveling chautauquas, the Great Plains Chautauqua Society is probably the most authentic. Founded in 1980 it was planned as a showcase for the humanities in which serious scholars would speak to community audiences as historical figures. Serving six midwestern states, it features the performances of scholars from the humanities who assume the

A Great Plains Chautauqua performance draws an overflow crowd. *Great Plains Chautauqua Society photo.*

roles of prominent personalities of the late nineteenth and early twentieth centuries.

Theodore Roosevelt, Jane Addams, Andrew Carnegie, Booker T. Washington, William Jennings Bryan, Henry David Thoreau, and Walt Whitman are among the many notable personalities who have been "brought to life" in the Great Plains Chautauqua programs. Like the tent chautauquas that proliferated across the country from 1904 to the early 1930s, the Great Plains programs are performed under large canvas tents, and like their original counterparts, they move from town to town for five-day stints.

With support from the National Endowment for the Humanities, their schedules include engagements in the smaller cities of North and South Dakota, Nebraska, Iowa, Kansas, and Oklahoma. The program's cultural thrust is centered on the scholars who assume the personas of the towering figures of their day, many of whom appeared in person on the chautauqua platforms of yesteryear. But the five-day offering includes much more. Interwoven with the impersonations are musical events, children's workshops, crafts demonstrations, nature walks, presentations by humorists, and worship services, all of which are related to a central theme.

Incorporating the nostalgia of the original tent chautauquas and drawing on the experience of the Chautauqua Institution, the Great Plains Chautauqua Society and other independents are responding to modern America's search for culture in an often confusing and complex world. Richie and Eben Schultz would be pleased to know that the romance of chautauqua is still alive in a thriving renaissance movement.

Appendix A

Historical Perspective of the Tent Chautauqua Era

1900 Theodore Roosevelt elected president of the United States.
1903 Orville Wright made the first successful flight in a heavier-than-air, mechanically propelled aircraft.
1904 Keith Vawter established the first traveling tent chautauqua circuit.
      Ida Tarbell published her muckraking *History of the Standard Oil Company*.
1906 San Francisco severely damaged by a devastating earthquake and fire.
1908 William Howard Taft elected president of the United States.
      Henry Ford introduced the Model T, which revolutionized the automobile industry.
1910 Boy Scouts of America founded.
1912 Woodrow Wilson elected president of the United States.
1914 Panama Canal officially opened.
      World War I broke out in Europe.
1915 First transcontinental telephone call, from New York to San Francisco, by Alexander Graham Bell and Thomas A. Watson.
1917 United States declared war on Germany.
      18th Amendment (Prohibition) passed by Congress and ratified the following year.
1918 Armistice signed, ending the war in Europe.
1920 Warren G. Harding elected president of the United States.
      19th Amendment ratified, giving women the right to vote.

1923 First sound-on-film motion picture, shown in New York's Rivoli Theater.

Calvin Coolidge became president of the United States upon the death of Warren G. Harding.

1927 Charles A. Lindbergh made the first solo flight across the Atlantic from New York to Paris.

1928 Herbert Hoover elected president of the United States.

1929 The stock market crashed, triggering the Great Depression.

1932 Franklin D. Roosevelt elected president of the United States.

Appendix B

Ellison-White Chautauqua Schedule, 1924

4/2–9 Abbeville, La.
3–10 Orange, Tex.
4–11 Fort Arthur, Tex.
5–12 Brenham, Tex.
(6)
7–14 Bryan, Tex.
8–15 Navasota, Tex.
9–16 Galveston, Tex.
10–17 Victoria, Tex.
11–18 Cuero, Tex.
12–19 Beeville, Tex.
(13)
14–21 Corpus Christi, Tex.
15–22 San Marcos, Tex.
16–23 New Braunfels, Tex.
17–24 Uvalde, Tex.
18–25 Del Rio, Tex.
19–26 Marfa, Tex.
(20)
21–28 El Paso, Tex.
22–29 (open)
23–30 Globe, Ariz.
24–1 Miami, Ariz.

25–2 Safford, Ariz.
27–2 Pearce, Ariz.
28–5 Mesa, Ariz.
29–6 Phoenix, Ariz.
30–7 Yuma, Ariz.
5/1–8 Redlands, Calif.
2–9 Riverside, Calif.
3–10 Azusa, Calif.
6–13 Pomona, Calif.
7–14 Alhambra, Calif.
8–15 Whittier, Calif.
9–16 Fullerton, Calif.
10–17 Santa Ana, Calif.
12–19 San Pedro, Calif.
13–20 Santa Barbara, Calif.
14–21 Glendale, Calif.
15–22 Bakersfield, Calif.
16–23 Porterville, Calif.
17–24 Lindsay, Calif.
(18)
19–26 Tulare, Calif.
20–27 Hanford, Calif.
21–28 Kingsburg, Calif.

22–29 Madera, Calif.
23–30 Turlock, Calif.
24–31 Modesto, Calif.
(25)
26–2 Stockton, Calif.
27–3 Lodi, Calif.
28–4 Los Gatos, Calif.
29–5 Palo Alto, Calif.
30–6 Petaluma, Calif.
31–7 Healdsburg, Calif.
6/(1)
2–9 Fortuna, Calif.
3–10 Eureka, Calif.
4–11 Willits, Calif.
5–12 Fort Bragg, Calif.
6–13 Ukiah, Calif.
7–14 Lakeport, Calif.
9–16 Sebastopol, Calif.
10–17 Santa Rosa, Calif.
11–18 Richmond, Calif.
12–19 Woodland, Calif.
13–20 Sacramento, Calif.
14–21 Reno, Nev.
16–23 Winnemucca, Nev.
17–24 Elko, Nev.
18–15 Ogden, Utah
19–26 Tooele, Utah
20–27 Preston, Idaho
21–28 Blackfoot, Idaho
23–30 Pocatello, Idaho
24–1 Burley, Idaho
26–3 Jerome, Idaho
27–4 Gooding, Idaho
28–5 Nampa, Idaho
(29)

30–7 Boise, Idaho
7/1–8 Caldwell, Idaho
2–9 Parma, Idaho
3–10 Weiser, Idaho
4–11 Baker, Oreg.
5–12 (open)
(6)
7–14 Colfax, Wash.
8–15 Lewiston, Wash.
9–16 Walla Walla, Wash.
10–17 Dallas, Oreg.
11–18 Corvallis, Oreg.
12–19 Roseburg, Oreg.
(13)
14–21 Eugene, Oreg.
15–22 Gladstone, Oreg.
16–23 Salem, Oreg.
17–24 Chevalis [*sic*], Wash.
18–25 Raymond, Wash.
19–26 Grays Harbor, Wash.
21–28 Olympia, Wash.
22–29 Puyallup, Wash.
23–30 Anacortes, Wash.
24–31 Bellingham, Wash.
25–1 Ellensburg, Wash.
26–2 Yakima, Wash.
28–4 Sunnyside, Wash.
29–5 Hilliard, Wash.
30–6 Missoula, Mont.
31–7 Hamilton, Mont.
8/1–8 Anaconda, Mont.
2–9 Dillon, Mont.
4–11 Bozeman, Mont.
5–12 Billings, Mont.
6–13 Roundup, Mont.

Appendix C

1925 Redpath Chautauqua Circuit

1925 SCHEDULE
REDPATH CHAUTAUQUAS
OF NEW YORK AND NEW ENGLAND

CRAWFORD A. PEFFER, MANAGER   WHITE PLAINS, NEW YORK

ITINERARY ....

1.	Niagara Falls, N. Y.	June	16	17	18	19	20	22
2.	Ransomville, N. Y.	June	17	18	19	20	22	23
3.	Attica, N. Y.	June	18	19	20	22	23	24
4.	Perry, N. Y.	June	19	20	22	23	24	25
5.	Arcade, N. Y.	June	20	22	23	24	25	26
6.	Dunkirk, N. Y.	June	22	23	24	25	26	27
7.	Batavia, N. Y.	June	23	24	25	26	27	29
8.	Akron, N. Y.	June	24	25	26	27	29	30
1.	Williamsville, N. Y.	June	25	26	27	29	30 July	1
2.	North Tonwanda, N. Y.	June	26	27	29	30 July	1	2
3.	Lockport, N. Y.	June	27	29	30 July	1	2	3
4.	Olcott, N. Y.	June	29	30 July	1	2	3	4
5.	Lyndonville, N. Y.	June	30 July	1	2	3	4	6
6.	Albion, N. Y.	July	1	2	3	4	6	7
7.	Brockport, N. Y.	July	2	3	4	6	7	8
8.	East Rochester, N. Y.	July	3	4	6	7	8	9
1.	Honeoye Falls, N. Y.	July	4	6	7	8	9	10
2.	Geneseo, N. Y.	July	6	7	8	9	10	11
3.	Canandiagua, N. Y.	July	7	8	9	10	11	13
4.	Naples, N. Y.	July	8	9	10	11	13	14
5.	Williamson, N. Y.	July	9	10	11	13	14	15
6.	Newark, N. Y.	July	10	11	13	14	15	16
7.	Clifton Springs, N. Y.	July	11	13	14	15	16	17
8.	Ovid, N. Y.	July	13	14	15	16	17	18
1.	Waterloo, N. Y.	July	14	15	16	17	18	20
2.	Moravia, N. Y.	July	15	16	17	18	20	21
3.	Cortland, N. Y.	July	16	17	18	20	21	22
4.	Cazenovia, N. Y.	July	17	18	20	21	22	23
5.	Hamilton, N. Y.	July	18	20	21	22	23	24
6.	Norwich, N. Y.	July	20	21	22	23	24	25
7.	Walton, N. Y.	July	21	22	23	24	25	27
8.	Oneonta. N. Y.	July	22	23	24	25	27	28
1.	Cobleskill, N. Y.	July	23	24	25	27	28	29
2.	Cooperstown, N. Y.	July	24	25	27	28	29	30
3.	Herkimer, N. Y.	July	25	27	28	29	30	31
4.	Dolgeville, N. Y.	July	27	28	29	30	31 Aug.	1
5.	Fort Plain, N. Y.	July	28	29	30	31 Aug.	1	3
6.	Oneida, N. Y.	July	29	30	31 Aug.	1	3	4
7.	Fulton, N. Y.	July	30	31 Aug.	1	3	4	5
8.	Wolcott, N. Y.	July	31 Aug.	1	3	4	5	6
1.	Oswego, N. Y.	Aug.	1	3	4	5	6	7
2.	Camden, N. Y.	Aug.	3	4	5	6	7	8
3.	Adams, N. Y.	Aug.	4	5	6	7	8	10
4.	Carthage, N. Y.	Aug.	5	6	7	8	10	11
5.	Theresa, N. Y.	Aug.	6	7	8	10	11	12
6.	Ogdensburg, N. Y.	Aug.	7	8	10	11	12	13
7.	Gouverneur, N. Y.	Aug.	8	10	11	12	13	14
8.	Potsdam, N. Y.	Aug.	10	11	12	13	14	15
1.	Massena, N. Y.	Aug.	11	12	13	14	15	17
2.	Malone, N. Y.	Aug.	12	13	14	15	17	18
3.	Tupper Lake, N. Y.	Aug.	13	14	15	17	18	19
4.	Saranac Lake, N. Y.	Aug.	14	15	17	18	19	20
5.	Plattsburg, N. Y.	Aug.	15	17	18	19	20	21
6.	Burlington, Vt.	Aug.	17	18	19	20	21	22
7.	Hardwick, Vt.	Aug.	18	19	20	21	22	24
8.	Montpelier, Vt.	Aug.	19	20	21	22	24	25
1.	Lyndonville, Vt.	Aug.	20	21	22	24	25	26
2.	Newport, Vt.	Aug.	21	22	24	25	26	27
3.	Woodsville, N. H.	Aug.	22	24	25	26	27	28
4.	Berlin, N. H.	Aug.	24	25	26	27	28	29
5.	Lancaster, N. H.	Aug.	25	26	27	28	29	31
6.	North Conway, N. H.	Aug.	26	27	28	29	31 Sept.	1
7.	Laconia, N. H.	Aug.	27	28	29	31 Sept.	1	2
8.	Portsmouth, N. H.	Aug.	28	29	31 Sept.	1	2	3
1.	Kennebunk, Me.	Aug.	29	31 Sept.	1	2	3	4
2.	Auburn, Me.	Aug.	31 Sept.	1	2	3	4	5
3.	Rumford, Me.	Sept.	1	2	3	4	5	7
4.	Farmington, Me.	Sept.	2	3	4	5	7	8
5.	Skowhegan, Me.	Sept.	3	4	5	7	8	9
6.	Waterville, Me.	Sept.	4	5	7	8	9	10

*Chautauqua Collection, Pelletier Library, Allegheny College, Meadville,
Pennsylvania.*

Appendix D

The Pollard Players' Schedule, 1927

ASSOCIATED CHAUTAUQUAS   SEASON 1927

The Pollard Players

PLAYING

"BELIEVE ME XANTIPPE"

May 9—Hagerman, N. M.
May 10—Elida, N. M.
May 11—Petersburg, Texas
May 12—Matador, Texas
May 13—Vera, Texas
May 14—McCaulley, Texas
May 15—Cranfills Gap, Texas
May 16—Blanco, Texas
May 17—Open
May 18—Open
May 19—Ozona, Texas
May 20—St. Stockton, Texas
May 21—Open
May 22—Open
May 26—Bowie, Arizona
May 27—Open
May 28—Wickenburg, Arizona
May 29—Open
May 30—Winslow, Ariz.
May 30—Open
June 1—Bishop, Cal.
June 2—Open
June 2—Westwood, Cal.
June 3—Cadora, Cal.
June 4—Weaverville, Cal.
June 5—Dorris, Cal.
June 6—Chiloquin, Ore.
June 7—Mitchell, Ore.
June 8—Burns, Ore.
June 9—Prairie City, Ore.
June 10—Heppner, Ore.
June 11—Enterprise, Ore.
June 12—Pasco, Wash.
June 13—St. John, Wash.
June 14—Culdesac, Idaho
June 15—Orofino, Idaho
June 16—Cottonwood, Idaho
June 17—Cambridge, Idaho
June 18—New Plymouth, Idaho
June 19—Kuna, Idaho
June 20—Meridian, Idaho
June 21—Jerome, Idaho
June 22—American Falls, Idaho
June 23—Aberdeen, Idaho
June 24—Ashton, Idaho
June 25—Driggs, Idaho
June 26, Jackson, Wyo.
June 27—Big Piney, Wyo.
June 28—Kemerer, Wyo.
June 29—Afton, Wyo.
June 30—Paris, Idaho
July 1—Grace, Idaho
July 2—Arimo, Idaho
July 3—Kimberly, Idaho
July 4—Parma, Idaho
July 5—Halfway, Ore.
July 6—Fossil, Ore.
July 7—White Salmon, Wash.
July 8—Newberg, Ore.
July 9—North Bend, Ore.
July 10—Sheridian, Wyo.

July 11—Forest Grove, Ore.
July 12—Open
July 13—Forks, Wash.
July 14—Sequini, Wash.
July 15—Edison, Wash.
July 16—Denning, Wash.
July 17—Open
July 18—Oaksdale, Wash.
July 19—Newport, Wash.
July 20—Bonners Ferry, Idaho
July 21—Polson, Montana
July 22—Stevensville, Montana
July 23—Philipsburg, Montana
July 24—Salmon, Idaho
July 25—Twin Bridges, Montana
July 26—Harrison, Montana
July 27—Townsend, Montana
July 28—St. Benton, Montana
July 29—Joplin, Montana
July 30—Harlem, Montana
July 31—Culbertson, Montana
Aug. 1—Medicine Lake, Montana
Aug. 2—Barnville, Montana
Aug. 3—Richey, Montana
Aug. 4—Circle, Montana
Aug. 5—Anndon, N. D.
Aug. 6—Rhome, N. D.
Aug. 7—Buffalo, S. D.
Aug. 8—Harden, Mont.
Aug. 9—Bridger, Mont.
Aug. 10—Camley, Wyo.
Aug. 11—Riverton, Wyo.
Aug. 12—Glenrock, Wyo.
Aug. 13—Lingle, Wyo.
Aug. 14—Imperial, Nebraska
Aug. 15—Wauneta, Nebraska
Aug. 16—Holbrook, Nebraska
Aug. 17—Agallah, Kansas
Aug. 18—Gorham, Kansas
Aug. 19—Greene, Kansas
Aug. 20—Axtell, Kansas
Aug. 21—Forbes, Missouri
Aug. 22—Fillmore, Missouri
Aug. 23—Reserve, Kansas
Aug. 24—Palmyra, Nebraska
Aug. 25—Elmwood, Nebraska
Aug. 26—Whiting, Iowa
Aug. 27—Pisgah, Iowa
Aug. 28—Denver, Missouri
Aug. 29—Ridgeway, Missouri
Aug. 30—New London, Missouri
Aug. 31—Tennessee, Ill.
Sept. 1—Redmon, Ill
Sept. 2—Heltonville, Indiana
Sept. 3—Clarksburg, Indiana
Sept. 4—New Castle, Kentucky
Sept. 5—Kyrock, Kentucky
Sept. 6—Open
Sept. 7—Morgantown, Kentucky
Sept. 8—Minor Hill, Tennessee
Sept. 9—Albany, Kentucky

Pat and Bill Kessler Chautauqua Collection.

Glossary

Richie Schultz drew on his experience with the Redpath-Vawter and New York–New England Chautauqua circuits to compile a list of chautauqua argot, which was published as an article, "Chautauqua Talk," in the August 1932 issue of *American Speech Magazine.* Following are edited excerpts from the article:

A-frame. The framework of heavy timbers in the form of a wide-spreading A placed at the junction of the "kitchen" with the main portion of the tent. It supported the proscenium of the stage.

Anvil chorus. The crew that set up, tore down, and maintained the tent and peripheral facilities.

Billboards. Small display boards that were placed about the town in strategic places with the announcements of the events of the day. These were changed each night by members of the crew. Also called "day boards."

Blow-down. The occasion of a tent being wrecked by a windstorm.

Bureau. The management; the office that directed one or more circuits.

Cashier. The woman or crewman who sold tickets and was in direct charge of the finances during the engagement in each town.

Circuit. A group of towns that were linked together to receive the programs in rotating order. One bureau might conduct several circuits.

Circuit manager. The overseer and troubleshooter of the entire circuit, who supervised the superintendents in charge of individual towns. Also called the "general superintendent."

Crew tent. A small tent at the rear of the main tent, behind the stage, used by the crew as living and sleeping quarters.

Diplomat. Any of the advance agents of the chautauqua. Frequently shortened to "dip."

Docott. A device of pulleys and ropes used to tighten the tent. Named in honor of a Dr. Ott, a lecturer who is said to have suggested the arrangement.

Double stake. In case of unfavorable grounds or a windy location, a tent might require extra stakes for the guy ropes, especially at the seams of the canvas.

Eight-day advance man. The agent, or "diplomat," who came into town to assist with the ticket sale during the week immediately preceding chautauqua.

Fence. A wide piece of canvas extending entirely around the big tent at some distance from it. The enclosure thus formed became the chautauqua grounds.

Field manager. The overseer of the advance work.

Fives. A circuit with a five-day program.

Gate. The entrance to the grounds, formed as a narrow passageway between two sections of fence extended beyond each other.

Guarantee. The amount of season tickets required to secure a chautauqua in the town. In common usage on the circuit, it was synonymous with "contract."

Hickey. A portion of a tent that had been tightened by pulling up slack on the guy ropes.

Junior supervisor. The young woman in charge of children's activities and programs. Also called the "story lady."

Junk. An inclusive term for all the chautauqua equipment. Used most frequently in drayage contracts, where the drayman received a certain amount for hauling the trunks, and a certain amount for the "junk."

Kitchen. The section of the tent that covered the stage. It also contained the dressing rooms.

Lazyback. A type of bench that was built on the grounds for audience members who carried only the canvas portions of their own chairs.

Local chairman. The head of the local chautauqua committee.

Local committee. The executive committee representing the signers of the chautauqua contract. Sometimes applied to the whole list of guarantors.

Make big. To be a big success.

Morning hour. Any program given in the morning. Originally this was a lecture or series of lectures. As chautauqua evolved, the morning hour was given over to children's programs.

Old folk's bench. A long wooden bench placed directly in front of the stage for the benefit of the elderly and those who were hard of hearing.

Property man. The crew foreman; often called the "prop."

Pup tent. A small tent at the rear of the stage used by the crew as living and sleeping quarters. Also called the "crew tent."

Prop trunk. The trunk in which the play or concert companies carried their properties. Also, the trunk in which the property man carried his tools and repair materials from town to town.

Pullman. The baggage car that was chartered to carry the chautauqua tent and equipment. Referred to as the "pullman" because the tent crew frequently slept in it as they moved from one town to another.

Reserves. Tickets for the reserved seat section. They were for the season or for single entertainments.

Seasons. Season tickets for admittance to all programs.

Sevens. A circuit with a seven-day program.

Smokers' bench. A bench (or benches) placed just outside the tent for those who wished to smoke during a program.

Supe. The superintendent who represented chautauqua management during the engagement in each town. Often called the "platform manager" because he made the announcements, introduced the speakers, and so on. It was his duty to keep the patrons interested on and off the platform. He supervised the crew and was in charge of moving the operation from one town to the next. He was also responsible for booking chautauqua for the following year.

Tack hammer. The large sledge with which stakes were driven.

Talent. A small tent at the rear of the stage used as a dressing room by the speakers and entertainers.

Tear-down. The operation of tearing down the tent. The night of the final performance was usually tear-down night.

Ticket booth. A small booth formed by canvas stretched around four metal uprights and roofed with canvas, from which tickets were sold. Occasionally the booth was a wooden structure. It was located just outside the grounds a short distance from the gate.

Twenty-one day advance man. An advance agent who moved on a three-day schedule, three weeks in advance of the opening of Chautauqua Week. His chief duty was to coordinate the advertising and generate interest in chautauqua, preparing the way for the later advance man.

Twilight circuit. A circuit whose programs were presented only in the evening.

Bibliography

Historical Archives

Bloomington Public Library, Historical Archives, Bloomington, Illinois.

Butler County Historical Society Archives, Butler, Pennsylvania.

Chautauqua Collection. Lawrence Pelletier Library, Allegheny College, Meadville, Pennsylvania.

Chautauqua Institution Archives. Chautauqua Institution, Chautauqua, New York.

"Chautauquas" (vertical file). Idaho State Historical Society Library Archives, Boise, Idaho.

Friends Historical Library, Special Collections. Swarthmore College, Swarthmore, Pennsylvania.

Lewis County Historical Society Archives, Canton, Missouri.

Ontario County Archive and Records Center, Canandaigua, New York.

Oregon Historical Society, Portland, Oregon.

Redpath Chautauqua Collection. Special Collections Department, University of Iowa Libraries, Iowa City, Iowa.

Publications

Case, Victoria, and Robert O. Case. *We Called It Chautauqua*. Garden City, N.J.: Doubleday, 1948.

DaBall, Irene Briggs, and Raymond F. DaBall. *Recollections of the Lyceum and Chautauqua Circuits.* Freeport, Maine: Bond Wheelwright, 1971.

Day, Beth. *The Little Professor of Piney Woods.* New York: Julien Messner, 1955.

Day, Louise, "My Chautauqua." *Idaho Yesterdays* 13, no. 3 (fall 1969): 2–5.

Dillavou, George J. "Swarthmore Chautauqua: An Adult Education Enterprise." Ph.D. diss., University of Chicago, 1970.

Duncan, Thomas W. *O, Chautauqua.* New York: Coward, McCann: 1935.

Fargo, Lucile F. *Prairie Chautauqua.* New York: Dodd, Mead: 1943.

Gould, Joseph E. *The Chautauqua Movement.* 1911. Reprint, Albany: State University of New York Press, 1972.

Graham, Donald L. "Aspects of the Chautauqua Movement in the Midwest." Ph.D. diss., University of Iowa, 1952.

Jameson, Sheilagh S. *Chautauqua in Canada.* Calgary: Glenbow-Alberta Institute, 1979.

Harrison, Harry P., as told to Karl Detzer. *Culture under Canvas.* New York: Hastings House, 1958; Westport, Conn.: Greenwood Press, 1978.

Henry Ford Museum and Greenfield Village Herald 13, no. 2. Dearborn, Mich.: Edison Institute, 1984.

Horner, Charles F. *The Life of James Redpath.* New York: Barse and Hopkins, 1926.

MacLaren, Gay. *Morally We Roll Along.* Boston: Little, Brown, 1938.

Mallett, Richard P. *The History of Farmington* [Maine]. N.p., 1992.

McCown, Robert A. "The Development of the Tent Chautauqua." *Henry Ford Museum and Greenfield Village Herald* 13, no. 2 (1984): 32–39.

Melzer, Richard. "Chautauquas: Caravans of Culture." *New Mexico Magazine,* September 1994, 56–63.

Miller, Brandon M. "When Chautauqua Came to Town." *Cobblestone Magazine,* July 1984, 39–41.

Miller, Katharine Aird, and Raymond H. Montgomery. *A Chautauqua to Remember.* Petersburg, Ill.: Silent River Press, 1987.

Moore, Victor Ivan. "The American Circuit Chautauqua: A Social Movement." Master's thesis, University of Texas, 1927.

Orchard, Hugh A. *Fifty Years of Chautauqua*. Cedar Rapids: Torch Press, 1923.

Schultz, John Richie. "Chautauqua Talk." *American Speech Magazine*, August 1932, 405–11.

Scott, Marion. *Chautauqua Caravan*. New York: Appleton-Century, 1939.

Tapia, John E. *Circuit Chautauqua*. Jefferson, N.C.: McFarland, 1997.

Tarbell, Ida M. *All in a Day's Work*. New York: Macmillan, 1939.

Wells, Carveth. *In Coldest Africa*. New York: Doubleday, Doran, 1929.

Acknowledgments

The inspiration for this book came from my father, the late John Richie Schultz, who with his brother, Eben, not only worked in the traveling chautauqua movement but also collected memorabilia and written accounts of the tent chautauqua experience. Most of his and Eben's collections reside in the archives of the Lawrence Pelletier Library at Allegheny College in Pennsylvania. I have retained a few items, including my father's notes for a book he was planning to write on the chautauqua movement before his premature death in 1947. Eben's daughter, June Schultz, also has some chautauqua materials, including personal recollections and photographs, which she generously made available for purposes of the book.

My invaluable assistant in conducting the research, critiquing the text, and developing the index has been my devoted wife, Dorothy. In addition to the contributions of my cousin June Schultz, my sister, Laurana Fish, stepped in to join our research efforts in the eastern part of the country. My daughter, Linda Robinson, and granddaughter Emily Robinson collaborated on the map of the Lake Chautauqua region.

At the outset of the project, I was encouraged by the late Alfreda Irwin, librarian and archivist at the Chautauqua Institution, who facilitated my research and gave valuable advice. Joyce Brasted, the current director of archives at the institution, has continued to be helpful. Connie Thorson, former librarian of Allegheny's Lawrence Pelletier

Library, was a big supporter and with her staff, including Joanne La-Tourette, helped to ferret out many items of interest from their chautauqua collection. Jane Westenfeld, of the Allegheny library staff, has more recently been helpful in providing additional materials from the Allegheny archives. Patricia O'Donnell, curator of the Friends Historical Library at Swarthmore College, enabled us to obtain materials from Swarthmore's chautauqua collection.

Robert A. McCown and Kathryn Hodson, of the University of Iowa Libraries, preside over the most extensive collection of circuit chautauqua materials in the country. As a recognized authority on circuit chautauqua history, Dr. McCown opened the door to the university archives and was kind enough to review a draft of my manuscript. Journalist Roberta Dodson and author Walter Truett Anderson also reviewed the manuscript, and both offered helpful advice. Tom McFarland, retired head of the university press based in Hanover, New Hampshire, also reviewed an early draft of the manuscript and made suggestions that sent me on a different and much improved tack.

I am particularly indebted to the editorial staff of the University of Missouri Press, including Beverly Jarrett, Jane Lago, and Julianna Schroeder, for their invaluable assistance and faith in the project.

Carol McCracken, granddaughter of chautauqua impresario Crawford Peffer, provided fresh information related to her grandfather's significant role in the circuit chautauqua movement. She also put me in touch with Pat Kessler, whose parents toured as actors on the chautauqua stage. Pat and her husband, Bill, contributed anecdotal materials and original photographs, considerably enhancing the tent chautauqua story. Dr. Matthew Little, chairman of the Department of English at the University of Mississippi, was helpful in providing authoritative assistance on language usage.

I am also indebted to a number of people who remembered chautauqua coming to their hometowns and shared their recollections of attending performances as children or young adults. Among them are Wesley Coe, who recalled the Mount Pleasant, Iowa, chautauqua as a highlight of his childhood; Austin Goforth, who traveled as a youngster with his father's popular band on a midwestern chautauqua circuit; J. H. Lindemuth, who attended chautauqua performances as a child in Mt. Joy, Pennsylvania; Richard P. Mallett of Farmington, Maine, who visited with presidential candidate Warren Harding when Harding spoke from the chautauqua platform in Farmington; and Kenneth Munford, who has vivid memories of attending the Ellison-White Chautauqua in his home state of Oregon. Helen Sandberg, Marge Hallock, Betty Fielding, and Miriam Mellon also reminisced with me about the chautauquas they attended as children.

Historical societies across the country went out of their way to respond to my requests for information about the tent chautauquas; among the many staff members who helped me are Judy Woodward and Jean Purvines of the Lewis County, Missouri, Historical Society; Mrs. Gerald B. "Jo" Morrow of the Macon, Missouri, Historical Society; Mary King, librarian of the Madison County Historical Society in Oneida, New York; Rebecca Sheeler of the Butler County, Pennsylvania, Historical Society; Troy Reeves of the Idaho State Historical Society; Judith Turner and Susan Otto of the Milwaukee Public Museum; Chad Wall of the Nebraska State Historical Society; Ed Varno and Preston Pierce of the Ontario County, New York, Historical Society; Elise Chan, curator of collections for the Jefferson County, New York, Historical Society; Richard Ingeman of the Oregon Historical Society; Lisa Hinzman of the State Historical Society of Wisconsin; Patricia Bakunas of the Richard J. Daley Library at the University of Illinois at Chicago; Terry Nichols of the State Historical Society of Missouri; Laura Bullion of the Western Historical Manuscript Collection–Columbia, Missouri; Duryea Kemp of the Ohio Historical Society; and Judith Kirsch of the Henry Ford Museum in Dearborn, Michigan. These individuals and their institutions graciously provided photographs, newspaper clippings, programs, posters, correspondence, and articles related to the traveling chautauquas.

It was gratifying to discover so much interest in a cultural movement that for the most part has been dormant for almost seventy years. I am deeply indebted to all who assisted in making my book a reality.

Index

Page numbers in italics are for illustrations.